D1541829

THE

weeknight

DESSERT

COOKBOOK

THE
weeknight
DESSERT
COOKBOOK

80 Irresistible Recipes with
Only 5 to 15 Minutes of Prep

Mary Younkin

Author of *The Weeknight Dinner Cookbook*
and creator of BarefeetInTheKitchen.com

PAGE STREET
PUBLISHING CO.

PAGE STREET
PUBLISHING CO.

Copyright © 2019 Mary Younkin

First published in 2019 by

Page Street Publishing Co.

27 Congress Street, Suite 105

Salem, MA 01970

www.pagestreetpublishing.com

All rights reserved. No part of this book may be reproduced or used, in any form or by any means, electronic or mechanical, without prior permission in writing from the publisher.

Distributed by Macmillan, sales in Canada by The Canadian Manda Group.

23   22   21   20   19   1   2   3   4   5

ISBN-13: 978-1-62414-859-0

ISBN-10: 1-62414-859-X

Library of Congress Control Number: 2018964665

Cover and book design by Ashley Tenn for Page Street Publishing Co.

Photography by Mary Younkin

Printed and bound in China

Page Street Publishing protects our planet by donating to nonprofits like The Trustees, which focuses on local land conservation.

For My Boys:

Sean, Sam, Ben, and Nate

Contents

IRRESISTIBLE ICE CREAMS, PUDDINGS, AND SAUCES 141

NO-BAKE TREATS FOR ANY SEASON 163

Introduction

You hold in your hands my forever favorite dessert recipes. These are the recipes I reach for time and time again, whether for a quick dessert after dinner or a fancier dessert for guests. With these recipes, you can pull together an amazing dessert in very little time at all.

The Weeknight Dessert Cookbook is filled with something for every craving: from cakes to cobblers, cookies to crisps, puddings to ice creams, no-bake treats, cookies, and more. This is where I've collected my tried-and-true dessert recipes for you.

Every recipe in this cookbook has been tested by me, of course, but they've also been tested by multiple volunteer home cooks just like you in a variety of kitchens. They are all reliable, delicious ways to satisfy your sweet tooth with approximately five to fifteen minutes of hands-on prep time.

What that five-to-fifteen-minute timeframe means is that all of your ingredients are ready and on the counter in front of you when you start the recipe. For example, the canisters of dry ingredients are on the counter, but not yet measured. The eggs, butter, and any additional ingredients are available at your fingertips as well.

That said, for most of these recipes, the five-to-fifteen-minute timeframe easily includes the moments required to assemble the ingredients. Over the years, I've found that measuring dry ingredients beforehand is unnecessary. While there are recipes that benefit from combining and sifting the dry ingredients first, those aren't the recipes in this book. I've streamlined the process here to eliminate that step.

Prepping the work area is key to making sure these really are quick and easy dessert recipes. Cleaning up along the way, dropping used tools in the sink, and wiping down the counter once the dessert is in the oven all help make sure that cleanup won't be a hassle.

BAKING TALK

Gas, electric, and convection ovens will all bake differently. I recommend using an oven thermometer to make sure you're actually baking at the recommended temperatures. Always test a cake before removing it from the oven.

To test for doneness, insert a bamboo skewer, toothpick, or butter knife straight into the center of the cake and lift it back out. If it comes out mostly clean with no wet batter sticking to it, the cake is done. If you can see wet batter clinging to the knife, the cake needs a few more minutes. Your patience will be rewarded.

Here are some constants to help you get consistent baking results for these recipes:

- Butter in my kitchen is always salted. Feel free to use unsalted if it is your preference. If you do prefer unsalted butter, just add a tiny pinch of salt to the recipe to replicate my results.

- Eggs are always large. This is a USDA regulated size. If you're in Europe or (lucky you!) have access to home-raised eggs, you're looking for 2-ounce (57-g) eggs.

- Measure carefully. Scoop flour and level with a knife.

- No liquor cabinet? No problem! You can find tiny bottles of different alcohols in most liquor stores. That is typically enough for most baking recipes.

To get the job done right, you need the right tools. Never fear, though, the tools for baking are, for the most part, ones you already have on hand or can get your hands on very inexpensively and easily. Here's a list of the most commonly used tools in *The Weeknight Dessert Cookbook*:

- First, you'll want an 8-inch (20-cm) pan, square or round. This is the perfect size to make just enough of a simple, everyday dessert. However, almost all the recipes in the book that use an 8-inch (20-cm) pan can be doubled for a 9 x 13–inch (23 x 33–cm) pan.

- A Bundt pan is also useful. Most of the recipes in this book use a half-size or 6-cup (1.4-L) Bundt pan, which is just enough dessert for one meal. The recipes can all be doubled for a standard-size Bundt pan.

- A loaf pan, typically about 6 cups (1.4 L) in size or approximately 5 x 8 inches (12 x 20 cm), is helpful, but if you have a half-size Bundt pan, it will do double duty for almost any recipe that calls for a loaf pan. That said, a loaf pan will not always work for the Bundt pan recipes.

- A baking sheet pan, half-sheet size, approximately 18 x 13 inches (46 x 33 cm), is a rimmed cookie sheet, and you'll use it endlessly.

- I use parchment paper or a silicone baking mat for almost everything I bake. Not only will parchment help with even cookie baking, but it also aids when lifting bars and bakes from the pan after baking. Nothing, and I do mean nothing, will stick to parchment.

- Last but not least, cookie scoops are indispensable in my kitchen. The convenience of scooping an entire tray of cookies in just a minute or two cannot be rated highly enough.

With the right tools and ingredients prepped, you'll be baking quickly in no time at all. None of these recipes are complicated or require hard-to-find ingredients, and all of them are guaranteed to end your meal on a lovely sweet note. Sharing my love of food and cooking for others are two of my favorite things. My hope is that this book brings you more joy in the kitchen and many happy memories shared with family and friends.

Mary Younkin

One-Pan Cakes for Every Occasion

If you love cake, and—even better—a fresh cake that requires little effort and provides big payoff, you will love that every one of the cakes in this book comes together with minimal hands-on time. The Mexican Chocolate Lava Cakes (page 27) take barely five minutes to stir together, and they're a showstopper of a dessert.

Craving chocolate? The Triple Chocolate Pound Cake (page 15) has your name on it. Do you love coffee? I mean, do you *really* love coffee? The Coffee Lovers' Cake (page 20) is a cake like nothing else I've ever tasted. I love it even more than I love my morning cup of coffee.

Want a dessert that looks like you spent some serious time in the kitchen, but truthfully requires no extra effort? Peach Upside-Down Cake (page 39) is what you're looking for. Do you know a coconut lover? The Best Ever Coconut Pound Cake (page 16) might make you their best friend.

Unless a recipe says differently, a toothpick inserted into a finished cake should come out with wet crumbs on it. If there is liquid or cake batter on the toothpick, it's not quite done, so bake for five to ten minutes longer and test again. These cakes can be stored at room temperature, loosely covered, preferably not in an airtight container.

CAKE TRANSFERRING

To transfer a cake from the pan it was baked in, place a plate that is large enough to overlap the pan by a couple of inches or a wire cooling rack over the cake, and then, holding the rack tightly over the cake by both sides, flip or invert the cake over the rack. The cake should fall from the pan at this point. If it does not, tapping the cake pan firmly with a wooden spoon should loosen it.

Baker's Note: If you don't see crumbs, the cake has likely overbaked. Don't worry, though. It'll still be tasty. Just drop a scoop of ice cream on top and say it was intentional, and then make a note for yourself for the next time you make it. It's all in how you sell it.

TRIPLE CHOCOLATE POUND CAKE

Yield: 6–8 servings, depending on size

Chocolate cake is a favorite dessert year-round, and this cake is one of the best. It's moist, tender, and filled with plenty of chocolate. It is almost chocolate overload, but a dark chocolate ganache frosting keeps it from being overly sweet. The coffee in this cake serves to intensify the chocolate flavor without adding a discernible coffee flavor to the finished cake.

FOR THE CAKE
½ cup (120 g) butter, softened, plus more for pan

¾ cup (150 g) light brown sugar

2 eggs

1 cup (240 ml) sour cream

1 cup (125 g) all-purpose flour

⅓ cup (35 g) regular or dark cocoa powder

1½ tsp (3 g) instant coffee

1 tsp baking soda

1 tsp baking powder

¼ tsp kosher salt

⅔ cup (112 g) dark or semi-sweet chocolate chips

FOR THE GANACHE
½ cup (84 g) dark or semi-sweet chocolate chips

3 tbsp (45 ml) heavy cream

Preheat the oven to 350°F (177°C). Thoroughly grease a 6-cup (1.4-L) loaf pan or mini Bundt pan with butter.

To make the cake, combine the butter and sugar in a large bowl. Beat with an electric mixer until smooth. Add the eggs and sour cream and beat again. Add the flour, cocoa powder, instant coffee, baking soda, baking powder, and salt. Beat until combined. Stir in the chocolate chips. The batter will be thick. Pour the batter into the prepared pan. Spread evenly with a spatula. Bake for 40 to 45 minutes, or until a toothpick inserted comes out clean or with moist crumbs.

Cool in the pan on a wire rack for 15 minutes. Then place a cooling rack on top of the cake, hold the sides firmly, and invert the pan over the rack. The cake should drop smoothly out of the pan. Let the cake cool completely.

To make the ganache, combine the chocolate chips and cream in a glass measuring cup or bowl. Microwave on full power for 90 seconds. Stir until smooth. Pour the ganache over the cake.

Baker's Notes: This cake doubles perfectly to fill a 12-cup (3-L) Bundt pan. I like to use both special dark cocoa powder and 60 percent dark chocolate chips in this cake. The darker chocolate deepens the flavor, and I especially love the ultra-dark color.

Add 1 tablespoon (15 ml) more of heavy cream to the ganache frosting to make it more pourable to drizzle over a Bundt cake.

Variation: Adding 1 tablespoon (4 g) of finely minced orange zest and ¼ cup (60 ml) of fresh orange juice to the batter takes this cake to a whole new level. We absolutely love the chocolate orange combination. If you do add the orange juice, reduce the sour cream to ¼ cup (58 g).

BEST EVER COCONUT POUND CAKE

Yield:
6–8 servings

I could quite possibly talk your ears off about how much I LOVE this coconut pound cake. The crumb is spectacular, the crust has the perfect crunch, and this beauty of a cake is drizzled with a sweet coconut icing and topped with an extra sprinkling of coconut. It's tender and fluffy enough for the perfect crumb, sweet but not overly sweet, with just the right amount of coconut flavor in every bite.

FOR THE CAKE
½ cup (120 g) butter, softened, plus more for pan

1 cup plus 2 tbsp (140 g) all-purpose flour, plus more for pan

1¼ cups (225 g) sugar

2 eggs

½ tsp vanilla extract

1 tsp coconut extract

¼ cup (60 ml) milk

½ tsp baking powder

¼ tsp kosher salt

½ cup (47 g) sweetened shredded coconut

FOR THE GLAZE
1 tbsp (14 g) butter, melted

¾ cup (75 g) powdered sugar

1 tbsp (15 ml) milk

½ tsp coconut extract

FOR THE TOPPING
⅓ cup (30 g) shredded sweetened coconut, toasted (optional)

Preheat the oven to 325°F (163°C). Arrange an oven rack in the center of the oven. Thoroughly grease and lightly flour a 6-cup (1.4-L) loaf pan or a mini Bundt pan.

To make the cake, combine the butter and sugar in a large bowl. Beat with an electric mixer until fluffy crumbs form. Add the eggs, vanilla, and coconut extract, and beat again until smooth. Add the milk and beat on low speed to combine. Add the flour, baking powder, and salt. Beat again, just until combined. Stir in the coconut.

Pour the batter into the prepared pan. Bake for 50 to 55 minutes, or until golden on top and light brown on the edges. A toothpick inserted should come out with moist crumbs. Cool in the pan on a wire rack for 15 minutes.

After 15 minutes, run a sharp knife around the edges of the cake pan and place the cooling rack on top of the cake, hold the sides firmly, and invert the pan over the rack. The cake should drop smoothly out of the pan. Tap firmly on the pan with a wooden spoon, if necessary, to free the cake from the pan. Let the cake cool completely before glazing.

To make the glaze, melt the butter in a small glass bowl. Add the powdered sugar, milk, and coconut extract. Whisk together until smooth. The glaze should pour off the spoon in a thick, white stream. Add 1 teaspoon or more of milk to thin it, or 1 to 2 tablespoons (7 to 13 g) of powdered sugar to thicken it, if necessary.

Drizzle the glaze over the cake. Sprinkle generously with shredded coconut, if desired. Store at room temperature, loosely covered, preferably not in an airtight container. This cake will keep nicely and stay very moist for 3 to 4 days.

Baker's Note: I'm not an advocate for buying a slew of specialty ingredients, but the coconut extract is key to the lovely flavor in this cake. Also, this recipe can be doubled to fill a 10-cup (2.6-L) Bundt pan. The Bundt cake will need to bake an additional 10 to 15 minutes.

STRAWBERRY-ALMOND COFFEE CAKE

Yield: 8–12 servings	This is a moist, berry-filled coffee cake with a hint of almond in the cake and a sprinkling of almonds on top. It's great with a cup of coffee in the morning or for dessert any night of the week. My youngest son loves this cake, and it's sure to be on his plate with his breakfast if there's a slice left over the next morning.

½ cup (120 g) butter, softened, plus more for pan

1 cup (200 g) white sugar

2 eggs

1 tsp vanilla extract

1 tsp almond extract

1 cup (125 g) all-purpose flour, divided

½ tsp baking powder

¼ cup (60 ml) sour cream

1½ cups (249 g) thinly sliced fresh strawberries

¼ cup (23 g) sliced almonds

1 tbsp (7 g) powdered sugar

Preheat the oven to 350°F (177°C). Grease an 8-inch (20-cm) round pan with butter.

Combine the butter and white sugar in a large bowl. Beat with an electric mixer for 3 to 4 minutes, or until light and fluffy. Stir in the eggs, vanilla, and almond extract. Add the flour, reserving 2 tablespoons (15 g), and baking powder and stir to combine. Mix in the sour cream.

Sprinkle the strawberries with the reserved flour and toss to coat. Gently stir the berries into the cake batter and scoop the batter into the prepared pan. Use a spatula to spread the batter in an even layer across the pan. Sprinkle the batter with the almonds.

Bake for 50 to 52 minutes, or until golden brown on top and a toothpick comes out with just a few moist crumbs. Let it cool completely before dusting with powdered sugar and slicing.

Baker's Notes: This cake also works well in a square pan or with other berries instead of strawberries. This cake, however, will not work with frozen berries, as they will add too much moisture to the cake. This is a very moist, almost dense, cake as written. You'll want to avoid adding any additional liquids or moisture to the batter.

You may be tempted to increase the berries in this cake, but I'll caution you not to do that. Too many berries will make it much harder to cook the cake all the way through, and it might be overly wet. Still tasty, but not the desired result.

COFFEE LOVERS' CAKE

Yield:
8–12 servings

The coffee in this recipe seasons both the cake and the frosting, cutting the sweetness of the cake without detracting from the fantastic flavor. But, you must like coffee . . . a lot. Fortunately, we do, and this is a very popular cake in our house.

Our friend Tom introduced us to this cake last year, and I couldn't get it out of my head. His version started with a cake mix and it was truly irresistible. So, I challenged myself to recreate it from scratch. This is truly a coffee lover's dream come true.

FOR THE CAKE
Butter, for greasing pan

1½ tsp (3 g) instant coffee

½ cup (120 ml) room-temperature water

½ cup (100 g) light brown sugar

¼ cup (50 g) white sugar

⅓ cup (80 ml) vegetable or light-flavored olive oil

2 eggs

1 tsp vanilla extract

1¼ cups (156 g) all-purpose flour

2 tsp (10 g) baking powder

½ tsp kosher salt

FOR THE FROSTING
1½ tsp (3 g) instant coffee

1 tbsp (15 ml) water

½ cup (120 g) butter, softened

2 cups (200 g) powdered sugar

½ tsp vanilla extract

2 tbsp (30 ml) heavy cream

Preheat the oven to 350°F (177°C). Grease an 8-inch (20-cm) round or square baking pan with butter.

To make the cake, combine the instant coffee and the water and stir to dissolve. Set aside.

Combine the light brown sugar, white sugar, and oil in a large bowl. Beat until fluffy crumbs form. Add the eggs and vanilla and beat to combine. Slowly pour in the coffee mixture while continuing to beat the mixture.

Slowly add the flour, baking powder, and salt to the egg mixture. Beat until just combined. Pour the batter into the prepared pan and bake for 34 to 36 minutes, or a toothpick comes out with just a few moist crumbs. Remove from the oven and cool completely before frosting.

To make the frosting, combine the instant coffee and the water and stir to dissolve. Place the butter in a bowl and beat with an electric mixer until smooth. Add the powdered sugar gradually, 1 cup (100 g) at a time, beating until well combined. Add the vanilla and the coffee, beating until well combined.

Slowly add the cream, while beating the frosting. The frosting should be light and fluffy. Spread the frosting over the cooled cake. Add more powdered sugar to the frosting for a thicker frosting or more cream for a thinner frosting.

Baker's Note: This cake can also be doubled for a 9 x 13–inch (23 x 33–cm) cake pan or made as a layer cake using two 8-inch (20-cm) round pans.

APPLE-RAISIN RUM CAKE

Yield:
12 servings

This is a lightly sweetened snackable cake that I cannot resist. The hint of flavor from the rum adds an extra depth to the overall flavor of this cake. Served on its own or with a dollop of whipped cream, this dessert is a hit.

Butter, for greasing pan

1½ cups (188 g) all-purpose flour

1½ tbsp (23 g) baking powder

¾ tsp ground cinnamon

¼ tsp ground ginger

¼ tsp kosher salt

½ cup (100 g) light brown sugar

1 egg

7 tbsp (105 ml) sour cream

½ cup (120 ml) applesauce

¼ cup (60 ml) golden or dark rum

½ cup (60 g) raisins

Whipped cream, for serving (optional)

Preheat the oven to 400°F (204°C). Grease an 8-inch (20-cm) square or round baking pan with butter.

In a medium bowl, whisk together the flour, baking powder, cinnamon, ginger, salt, and brown sugar.

In a large bowl, add the egg and sour cream. Whisk to combine. Add the applesauce and rum and whisk again until smooth. Add the dry ingredients to the wet ingredients and stir just until combined. Stir in the raisins.

Scrape the batter into the prepared baking pan. Bake for 25 minutes, or until the cake is golden brown and a toothpick inserted comes out mostly clean. Serve plain or with lightly sweetened whipped cream.

Baker's Notes: I like to use a mix of California raisins and golden raisins for this recipe. Any raisin you enjoy eating will work well with this cake.

The recipe can be doubled for a 9 x 13–inch (23 x 33–cm) or Bundt cake. Adjust the baking time as needed.

The rum in this recipe may be skipped if you'd prefer not to use any alcohol. You'll want to increase the applesauce to ⅔ cup (160 ml) if eliminating the rum.

BROWN SUGAR AND SPICE POUND CAKE

Yield:
8–12 servings

This cake is filled with spices, rich with butter and brown sugar, and just dense enough that you can slice it into super-thin snackable slivers without the cake falling apart. If this cake is in the house, I absolutely cannot resist it. With a cup of coffee or a glass of milk, this cake is spectacular.

¾ cup (180 g) butter, softened, plus more for the pan

1½ cups (188 g) all-purpose flour, plus more for the pan

1 cup (200 g) light brown sugar

½ cup (100 g) white sugar

2 eggs

1 tsp vanilla extract

1 tsp ground cinnamon

½ tsp ground ginger

¼ tsp ground nutmeg

¼ tsp ground cloves

½ tsp baking powder

¼ tsp kosher salt

½ cup (120 ml) milk

1 cup (150 g) chopped pecans (optional)

Preheat the oven to 325°F (163°C). Generously grease and flour a loaf pan or mini 6-cup (1.4-L) Bundt pan.

Combine the butter, brown sugar, and white sugar in a large bowl. Beat with an electric mixer until fluffy. Add the eggs and the vanilla. Beat to combine. Add the flour, cinnamon, ginger, nutmeg, cloves, baking powder, and salt. Beat to combine. Add the milk slowly while continuing to mix the batter. Stir in the pecans, if using.

Spoon the batter into the prepared pan and bake for 48 to 55 minutes, or until a toothpick comes out clean. Cool the cake in the pan for 10 minutes, before running a knife around the edge of the pan and then inverting the cake over a wire cooling rack. Cool completely before slicing.

Baker's Note: This recipe may be doubled to fill a 10- to 12-cup (2.6- to 3-L) Bundt pan. Depending on the type of pan you use, this may require additional baking time. Test for doneness with a toothpick and adjust accordingly. A mini Bundt pan will cook a few minutes faster than a loaf pan. A full-size Bundt pan may require a few extra minutes.

MEXICAN CHOCOLATE LAVA CAKES

Yield:
4 ramekins (5–6 ounces [150–180 ml]) or 6 ramekins (3–4 ounces [90–120 ml])

Lava cakes are a chocolate lover's dream come true. With a gooey center and a crackling crust, there is no other dessert that compares. This lava cake takes the original to a new level with a sprinkling of cinnamon and a pinch of hot pepper. That tiny bit of heat kicks up all of the flavors. I highly recommend topping these cakes with chocolate or cinnamon ice cream right before serving.

½ cup (120 g) butter, plus more for the pan

½ cup plus 2 tbsp (105 g) semi-sweet or dark chocolate chips

¾ cup (75 g) powdered sugar

1 tsp cinnamon

⅛–¼ tsp cayenne pepper

2 eggs

7 tbsp (56 g) cornstarch

Ice cream, for serving

Preheat the oven to 400°F (204°C). Place the ramekins on a baking sheet and grease the cups with butter or baking spray.

In a medium glass bowl, combine the butter and chocolate chips. Microwave or melt in a double boiler, until the butter has melted, about 1 minute in most microwaves or 3 to 5 minutes in a double boiler. Remove from the heat and stir to melt the chocolate completely.

Add the powdered sugar, cinnamon, and cayenne pepper to the chocolate mixture and stir to combine. Add the eggs and whisk until completely smooth. Add the cornstarch and stir until well combined.

Divide the batter between the greased cups. Bake for 16 to 18 minutes, or until the edges of each cup are firm and the center is still soft and liquid. Let the cakes cool for 5 minutes, and then top each serving with ice cream and serve immediately.

Baker's Note: We enjoy this recipe with ¼ teaspoon of cayenne pepper in the recipe. However, if you are leery of the heat and just want to punch up the flavor a bit, start with a scant ⅛ teaspoon of cayenne.

FLUFFY ZUCCHINI-LEMON CAKE

Yield:
12 servings

When zucchini is in abundance, there is endless potential for using this great vegetable. If you are already a fan of zucchini bread, I'd like to introduce you to zucchini cake. This is a fluffy lemon cake with specks of zucchini throughout.

This cake is perfect for snacking. I like to leave a butter knife in the pan, just to make it easy to slice slivers off of it. The sweet glaze nicely balances the tartness of this cake. Not overly sweet, with hints of zucchini and lemon throughout, this is the cake that might even convert zucchini haters into fans of the bountiful green vegetable.

FOR THE CAKE
1 medium-large Italian zucchini, grated (approximately 1½ cups [225 g])

¾ cup (150 g) sugar

2 eggs

½ cup (120 g) butter, melted

1 tsp vanilla extract

⅔ cup (160 ml) fresh lemon juice (approximately 5 large lemons)

2 cups (250 g) all-purpose flour

1½ tsp (8 g) baking powder

1 tsp baking soda

¼ tsp kosher salt

FOR THE GLAZE
3 tbsp (45 ml) fresh lemon juice (approximately ½ lemon)

1 cup (100 g) powdered sugar

Preheat the oven to 350°F (177°C). Grease an 8-inch (20-cm) round pan. Line a bowl with a triple layer of paper towels.

To make the cake, grate the zucchini and place it in the bowl with the paper towels. Use the paper towels to squeeze liquid from the shredded zucchini. Discard the liquid and place a clean paper towel in the bowl. Transfer the squeezed zucchini to the dry towel and let it rest for a few minutes.

In a medium bowl, whisk together the sugar and the eggs. Whisk in the butter, vanilla, and lemon juice. Add the flour, baking powder, baking soda, and salt. Stir to combine. Add the zucchini and stir once more. Pour into the greased pan. Bake for 40 to 45 minutes, or until golden brown and an inserted toothpick comes out clean. Remove from the oven and cool completely.

To make the glaze, whisk the lemon juice into the powdered sugar. Pour the glaze over the cooled cake.

Baker's Notes: You can flip the cooled cake onto a cake plate for serving or serve the cake directly from the pan. Either method will work fine; you can glaze the cake in the pan or on the platter.

Please note that there is a good amount of lemon juice in this cake. The cake is supposed to be fairly tart. If you prefer it a bit sweeter, increase the sugar to 1 cup (200 g). Also, the importance of fresh lemon juice versus bottled juice cannot be overstated here.

CHUNKY MONKEY SNACK CAKE

Yield:
9–12 servings

This Chunky Monkey Snack Cake is a rich banana cake filled with chopped pecans and a whole lot of chocolate. No frosting is needed, just bring a craving for a sweet snack cake. This cake is perfect with a glass of milk for an afternoon snack. (I recommend it for breakfast, too!) Or serve it warm with a scoop of vanilla ice cream and maybe even a drizzle of chocolate for a great dessert.

I've made this cake both with and without the chocolate chips and/or the nuts and while my personal preference is with the chocolate and nuts, the banana cake is wonderfully light and fluffy and completely delicious on its own.

½ cup (120 g) butter, softened, plus more for pan

⅔ cup (135 g) light brown sugar

½ cup (120 ml) sour cream

1 tbsp (15 ml) vanilla extract

1 egg

1 cup (125 g) all-purpose flour

1 tsp baking soda

¼ tsp kosher salt

3 small ripe bananas, mashed (approximately 1 cup [225 g])

½ cup (84 g) semi-sweet chocolate chips

⅓ cup (56 g) white chocolate chips

½ cup (60 g) chopped pecans or walnuts

Preheat the oven to 350°F (177°C). Grease an 8 x 8–inch (20 x 20–cm) pan with butter or line it with parchment paper.

Combine the butter and sugar together in a large bowl. Beat with an electric mixer until it forms fluffy crumbs. Add the sour cream and beat to combine. Add the vanilla and egg, and beat. Add the flour, baking soda, and salt, and beat just until combined. Stir in the bananas, and then add the semi-sweet and white chocolate chips and nuts.

Pour the batter into the prepared pan. Bake in the center of the oven for 32 to 36 minutes, or until the cake is golden brown and rounded on top and a toothpick comes out mostly clean with wet crumbs. Let it cool completely before slicing.

Baker's Note: Seriously ripe bananas with plenty of brown spots (the more the better) are the secret to rich and flavorful banana-flavored baked goods. I place the ripe bananas on a plate and use a fork to smash them. (This is my eight-year-old's favorite job in the kitchen.)

BUTTERY ALMOND POUND CAKE

Yield:
6–8 servings

This beauty of a pound cake is rich and buttery with a golden-brown crust. This cake is not overly sweet, and it's loaded with almond flavor.

I like to make this cake for a casual coffee break with friends, but it's certainly worthy of a company dinner as well. For a fancier dessert, the optional glaze dresses it up nicely.

FOR THE CAKE
½ cup (120 g) butter, softened, plus more for pan

1¼ cups (156 g) all-purpose flour, plus more for pan

1¼ cups (225 g) sugar

2 eggs

1½ tsp (7 ml) almond extract

¼ cup (60 ml) milk

½ tsp baking powder

¼ tsp kosher salt

FOR THE GLAZE (OPTIONAL)
1 tbsp (14 g) butter, melted

1 cup (100 g) powdered sugar

1½ tbsp (23 ml) milk

½ tsp almond extract

½ cup (50 g) sliced almonds (optional)

Preheat the oven to 325°F (163°C). Arrange an oven rack in the center of the oven. Thoroughly grease and lightly flour a 6-cup (1.4-L) loaf pan or mini Bundt pan with butter.

To make the cake, combine the butter and sugar together in a large bowl. Beat with an electric mixer until fluffy crumbs form. Add the eggs and almond extract and beat until smooth. Add the milk and beat on low speed to combine. Add the flour, baking powder, and salt. Beat until just combined.

Pour the batter into the prepared pan. Bake for 45 to 55 minutes, or until golden on top and light brown on the edges. Cool in the pan on a wire rack for 15 minutes. Then place the cooling rack on top of the cake, hold the sides firmly, and invert the pan over the rack. The cake should drop smoothly out of the pan. Tap firmly on the pan with a wooden spoon, if necessary, to free the cake from the pan. Let the cake cool completely before slicing.

If you'd like to make the glaze, melt the butter in a small glass bowl in the microwave, about 15 seconds. Add the powdered sugar, milk, and almond extract. Whisk together until smooth. The glaze should pour off the spoon in a white stream. Add 1 teaspoon more of milk to thin it, or 1 to 2 tablespoons (7 to 13 g) more of powdered sugar to thicken it, if necessary. Drizzle the glaze over the cake. Sprinkle with the almonds, if desired.

PINEAPPLE-COCONUT COFFEE CAKE

Yield: 9–12 servings	Pineapple and coconut are awesome together, and this super-moist coffee cake shows the pairing off nicely. Layered with a pineapple-coconut filling and then topped with a lime glaze and toasted coconut after it comes out of the oven, this is a whole new kind of coffee cake. If you enjoy the combination of coconut and pineapple, you're sure to love this dessert.

FOR THE CAKE

½ cup (120 g) butter, softened, plus more for pan

1 cup (200 g) white sugar

2 eggs

1 tsp vanilla extract

1 cup (125 g) all-purpose flour

½ tsp baking powder

½ cup (120 ml) sour cream

FOR THE PINEAPPLE FILLING

1 tbsp (15 ml) vanilla extract

2 tbsp (30 ml) fresh lime juice (approximately 1 large lime)

⅓ cup (67 g) light brown sugar

¼ cup (31 g) all-purpose flour

¼ tsp kosher salt

1 cup (165 g) pineapple chunks in 100 percent juice, drained very well in a strainer

1 cup (93 g) shredded sweetened coconut

FOR THE GLAZE

⅔ cup (56 g) powdered sugar

1 tbsp (15 ml) fresh lime juice

½ cup (47 g) shredded sweetened coconut, toasted, if desired

Preheat the oven to 350°F (177°C). Grease a 10-inch (25-cm) square baking dish with butter or line with parchment.

To make the cake, combine the butter and white sugar together in a large bowl. Beat with an electric mixer for 3 to 4 minutes, or until light and fluffy. Stir in the eggs and vanilla. Add the flour and baking powder and stir to combine. Mix in the sour cream. Pour half of the batter into the prepared pan. Make sure to spread it evenly across the bottom of the pan.

To make the pineapple filling, combine the vanilla, lime juice, brown sugar, flour, and salt in a large bowl. Stir to mix. Add the pineapple and coconut and stir to combine. Pour the pineapple filling over the batter in the pan and spoon the remaining batter over the pineapple layer. Smooth lightly with a spatula.

Bake for 35 to 38 minutes, or until golden brown and a toothpick comes out from the center with moist crumbs and pineapple juice. Let the cake cool completely.

To make the glaze, add the powdered sugar and lime juice to a small cup or bowl. Whisk together until smooth. The glaze should pour off a spoon in a thin, white stream. Add 1 teaspoon or more of lime juice to thin it or 1 to 2 tablespoons (7 to 13 g) more of the powdered sugar to thicken it, if necessary.

Pour the glaze over the cooled cake. Sprinkle generously with the shredded coconut. Store at room temperature, loosely covered.

Baker's Note: Any 2- to 2.5-quart (1.9- to 2.4-L) glass or ceramic baking dish will work for this cake. I've used an 8 x 10–inch (20 x 25–cm) glass dish and a round baking dish, as well. I do not recommend a metal baking pan for this recipe.

CRANBERRY COFFEE CAKE

<table>
<tr><td>Yield:
9–12 servings</td><td>Sweetly tart cranberries are mixed into an incredibly moist coffee cake that is slightly lemony and topped with a buttery brown sugar streusel. This is not an overly sweet or fluffy cake. It's a richly dense coffee cake with a lovely tartness from the cranberries.</td></tr>
</table>

FOR THE CAKE
½ cup (120 g) butter, softened, plus more for pan

1 cup (200 g) white sugar

2 eggs

2 tbsp (30 ml) fresh lemon juice (approximately ½ lemon)

2 tsp (10 ml) vanilla extract

1 cup plus 1 tbsp (133 g) all-purpose flour

½ tsp baking powder

1 cup (140 g) fresh cranberries

½ cup (120 ml) sour cream

FOR THE TOPPING
⅔ cup (83 g) all-purpose flour

⅓ cup (67 g) brown sugar

¼ cup (59 ml) melted butter

Preheat the oven to 350°F (177°C). Grease an 8-inch (20-cm) square pan with butter.

To make the cake, combine the butter and white sugar in a large bowl. Beat with an electric mixer for approximately 3 minutes, or until light and fluffy. Add the eggs, lemon juice, and vanilla, and mix until just combined.

In a medium bowl, combine 1 cup (125 g) of the flour and the baking powder.

Place the cranberries in a separate bowl and sprinkle with the remaining 1 tablespoon (8 g) of flour, stirring gently to coat the berries. Add half of the dry ingredients to the wet ingredients and stir to combine. Add the sour cream, mix again, and add the remaining dry ingredients. Mix until just combined. Gently stir in the cranberries and pour the batter into the prepared pan.

To make the topping, place the flour and sugar in the same small bowl that was holding the berries and add the melted butter. Stir lightly with a fork to combine. Sprinkle the sugary crumbs over the batter in the pan.

Bake for 42 to 46 minutes, or until a toothpick comes out clean or with moist crumbs. Let it cool completely before slicing.

Baker's Note: If cranberries are not in season, or if you do not currently have them stashed in your freezer, this cake will work nicely with blueberries as well. Frozen berries may be stirred into the batter straight from the freezer.

PEACH UPSIDE-DOWN CAKE

Yield:
8 servings

Warm, caramelized peaches over tender, lightly spiced cake is a dessert that I cannot resist. I typically serve this dessert warm topped with whipped cream or ice cream. This is a dessert best served warm from the oven. It won't be nearly as lovely the next day.

2 cups (500 g) partially thawed frozen peach slices

½ cup (120 g) butter, softened, plus more for pan

½ cup (120 ml) Salted-Vanilla Caramel Sauce (page 159) (store-bought is fine)

1 cup (200 g) white sugar

2 large eggs

1 tsp vanilla extract

1½ cups (188 g) all-purpose flour

2 tsp (10 g) baking powder

¾ tsp ground cinnamon

¼ tsp salt

½ cup (120 ml) milk

Whipped cream or ice cream, for serving

Preheat the oven to 350°F (177°C). Set the frozen peaches on the counter, so that they will thaw enough to break them apart. Grease an 8-inch (20-cm) round cake pan with butter.

Pour the caramel sauce into the bottom of the prepared pan and swirl to coat. Arrange the peach slices over the caramel in a single layer.

In a medium bowl, combine the butter and sugar. Beat with an electric mixer until light and fluffy. Add the eggs and vanilla. Beat until smooth. Add the flour, baking powder, cinnamon, and salt. Beat to combine. Add the milk while beating slowly, until just blended.

Pour the batter over the peach slices and spread evenly. Bake for 50 to 55 minutes, or until the top is a deep golden brown and a tester comes out clean. The cake should not shake or wobble when removed from the oven.

Let the cake cool in the pan for 5 minutes before using hot pads to carefully place a plate over the pan and then invert the cake onto the plate. Be careful to keep the plate and pan firmly pressed together while turning. Replace any peaches that might have stuck to the bottom of the pan. Serve warm with whipped cream or ice cream.

Baker's Note: Feel free to make this with fresh peaches when they're in season. However, with my year-round cravings for peaches, this is most frequently made with frozen fruit.

CHOCOLATE-CARAMEL PECAN POUND CAKE

Yield:
8–10 servings

This brown sugar pound cake is filled with melted caramel, chocolate chips, and pecans. It's baked until the sugared crust is deeply browned and crisp, and then it's topped with a thick chocolate glaze. A small slice is the perfect serving size for me, but I can never resist going back for just one more sliver for as long as the cake lasts in my kitchen. I love serving this rich cake with hot coffee or a tall glass of milk for the younger and non-coffee-drinking crowd.

FOR THE CAKE
¾ cup (180 g) butter, softened, plus more for pan

4 tbsp (50 g) white sugar, plus more to coat the loaf pan

1 cup (200 g) light brown sugar

1 tsp vanilla extract

2 eggs

½ cup (120 ml) milk

1½ cups (188 g) all-purpose flour

½ tsp baking powder

¼ tsp kosher salt

¾ cup (126 g) semi-sweet chocolate chips

⅓ cup (37 g) chopped pecans

⅓ cup (56 g) caramel bits (see Baker's Notes)

FOR THE FROSTING
1 cup (168 g) semi-sweet chocolate chips

¼ cup (60 g) butter

Preheat the oven to 325°F (163°C). Generously grease and sugar a 6-cup (1.4-L) loaf pan. Sprinkle the buttered pan with white sugar to coat thoroughly.

To make the cake, combine the butter, white sugar and brown sugar in a large bowl. Beat with an electric mixer until fluffy. Add the vanilla and then the eggs and beat well to combine. Slowly add the milk while beating.

Add the flour, baking powder, and salt and beat until just combined. Stir in the chocolate chips and pecans. Spoon the batter into the prepared pan. Sprinkle with the caramel bits and gently stir in with a knife or the end of a spoon.

Bake for 75 to 80 minutes, or until a toothpick comes out clean. Cool the cake in the pan for at least 15 minutes. Slide a sharp knife around the pan before inverting it over a cooling rack or cake plate. Cool completely before topping with chocolate frosting.

To make the frosting, combine the chocolate chips and the butter in a glass bowl. Microwave for 90 seconds. Stir until all of the chips have dissolved. Pour the warm frosting over the cake.

Baker's Notes: Please note that the recipe is very specific about how to add the caramel bits. If you stir in the caramel too early, the caramel bits will cause the cake to stick to the pan if too much of the caramel winds up at the sides and bottom of the batter in the pan.

This cake will very generously fill the loaf pan, but the cake does not rise too much and should not overflow. You can easily double this recipe using a 12-cup (3-L) Bundt pan. This cake will keep nicely for several days.

TANGY LIME CAKE WITH LIME–WHIPPED CREAM TOPPING

Yield: 4–5 servings	This tangy lime cake is irresistible for any lime lover. I can guarantee you rave reviews from anyone who enjoys the tart tanginess of fresh limes. The recipe makes a small cake, perfect for dessert for just a few people. If you'd like dessert for more people, or want to have a few extra slices, double the recipe and use a standard-size Bundt pan.

FOR THE CAKE

6 tbsp (90 g) butter, softened, plus more for pan

1 cup plus 2 tbsp (140 g) all-purpose flour, plus more for pan

1¼ cups (225 g) white sugar

¼ cup (16 g) lime zest (approximately 4 limes)

2 large eggs

1 tsp vanilla extract

⅓ cup (80 ml) fresh lime juice (approximately 3–6 medium limes)

½ tsp baking powder

½ tsp kosher salt

FOR THE LIME WHIPPED CREAM

4 oz (113 g) cream cheese, room temperature

2 tbsp (30 ml) fresh lime juice

1 cup (100 g) powdered sugar

1 tsp very finely minced lime zest

½ cup (120 ml) heavy cream

Fresh berries, for serving (optional)

Preheat the oven to 350°F (177°C). Generously grease and flour a small 6-cup (1.4-L) Bundt pan.

To make the cake, combine the white sugar with the lime zest in a large bowl. Rub the sugar mixture with your fingers for about 1 minute, or until the zest is evenly distributed through the sugar. Add the butter and beat with a mixer until fluffy crumbs form. Add the eggs, vanilla, and lime juice. Beat to combine. Add the flour, baking powder, and salt. Beat to combine.

Pour the batter into the prepared pan. Bake for about 40 to 45 minutes, or until a toothpick inserted comes out mostly clean or with crumbs. Cool for 5 minutes in the pan and then invert on a wire rack to cool completely.

To make the whipped cream, combine the cream cheese and the lime juice in a medium bowl. Beat to combine. Add the powdered sugar and lime zest. Beat until smooth. Slowly add the cream while beating constantly with an electric mixer or the whisk attachment on a stand mixer. Beat until smooth and creamy, about 2 minutes, and then continue beating for an additional 2 to 3 minutes, or until the mixture is fluffy.

Scoop the whipped cream into an airtight container and store in the refrigerator until ready to use. Top each slice of cake with whipped cream before serving. Serve with fresh berries, if desired.

Baker's Notes: The lime whipped cream can be made ahead of time and stored in the refrigerator. It will keep nicely for 3 to 4 days.

This recipe may be doubled to fill a standard 10- to 12-cup (2.6- to 3-L) Bundt pan. Increase the baking time by 10 to 15 minutes for the larger cake pan.

Cookie Recipes You'll Make on Repeat

Handheld, portable, and delicious, cookies are a great way to make a dessert that holds well for a couple of days and packs easily into lunches. Crispy Chocolate-Toffee Cookies (page 83), Lemon Poppy Seed Cookies (page 48), Almond Lovers' Crinkle Cookies (page 64), and Little Bit Salty, Little Bit Sweet Skillet Cookies (page 59) are just a few of the amazing cookie recipes that are waiting for you in this chapter.

Cookie baking is made far easier with cookie scoops. I use the following cookie scoops:

- #20: approximately 2 inches (5 cm) or 3 tablespoons (45 g)

- #40: approximately 1½ inches (4 cm) or 2 tablespoons (30 g)

- #50: approximately 1 inch (2.5 cm) or 1 tablespoon (15 g)

I own all three cookie scoop sizes and I use them all on a regular basis. If you're only buying one cookie scoop, the cookie scoop I use the most often is the #40 or 2-tablespoon (30-g) scoop.

PLEASE use parchment paper or a silicone mat to line your pan. This will prevent the disappointment of having to chisel your beautiful cookies from a pan that just doesn't want to give them up.

Let them breathe! Make sure you leave the amount of room between the cookies that is specified in the recipe. Most cookies will spread as they bake, and you want to be sure there is enough room for air to circulate around them.

Cookie dough freezes quite well, and I love to stash it away for late night cravings. There are a couple of different ways that you can freeze the dough.

OPTION 1: Simply transfer the dough to a freezer-safe resealable bag and press it flat. When you are ready to make the cookies, let the dough warm on the counter until it is soft enough to scoop.

OPTION 2: This option will satisfy those cravings even faster. Scoop the prepared cookie dough out onto a parchment-lined pan. You don't need to leave much room between them for this, because you'll just slide the pan into the freezer instead of the oven. When the cookie dough mounds are frozen solid, transfer them to a freezer bag labeled with the baking instructions and keep in the freezer for up to three months.

With the pre-scooped balls of cookie dough, you will be able to bake as many or as few cookies as you'd like on demand. You can bake the frozen cookie dough straight from the freezer, just add a few minutes to the baking time. These cookies will keep nicely for two to three days when stored in an airtight container at room temperature. They will also keep nicely in the freezer for up to three months.

GIANT COCONUT-PECAN CHOCOLATE CHUNK COOKIES

<table>
<tr><td>Yield:
6 (5–6"
[13–15-cm])
cookies or 18
(3" [8-cm])
cookies</td><td>These chewy chocolate, coconut, and pecan–filled cookies are going to satisfy all your cookie cravings. This recipe is designed to make GIANT cookies, and trust me, they're a treat. However, if you're in the mood for something a little more bite-sized, it will also make perfect smaller cookies.</td></tr>
</table>

¾ cup plus 2 tbsp (175 g) light brown sugar

½ cup (120 g) butter, melted

1 egg yolk

1½ tsp (7 ml) vanilla extract

1 cup (125 g) all-purpose flour

¼ tsp baking soda

¼ tsp kosher salt

½ cup (40 g) old-fashioned rolled oats

½ cup (55 g) roughly chopped pecans

½ cup (47 g) shredded sweetened coconut

⅔ cup (112 g) chocolate chunks or semi-sweet chocolate chips

Preheat the oven to 325°F (163°C). Line a baking sheet with parchment paper or a silicone mat.

Place the sugar in a large bowl. Add the hot melted butter and beat until smooth. Add the egg yolk and vanilla and beat again to combine. Add the flour, baking soda, salt, and oats and beat to combine. Add the pecans and coconut to the batter and stir well. Add the chocolate and stir to mix everything throughout the dough.

Divide the dough into 6 giant cookie dough balls and place 3 of the cookie dough balls on the prepared baking sheet. Leave a few inches between each cookie.

Bake the larger cookies for 15 to 16 minutes. Smaller cookies only need to bake for 11 to 12 minutes. Remove from the oven before the edges of the cookies have browned. The cookies should be puffy and cracked across the top.

Let them cool for 1 to 2 minutes on the baking sheet and then remove to a wire rack. Repeat with the rest of the dough. When the cookies have completely cooled, store in an airtight container.

Baker's Note: Do not refrigerate this dough before baking. The dough is very thick, and it will be rock-firm once cold. If you do need to chill the dough before baking the cookies, let it come to room temperature again before baking.

LEMON POPPY SEED COOKIES

Yield:
12–14
(4" [10-cm])
cookies

Chewy, buttery lemon cookies with crisp edges and plenty of poppy seeds are a winner. These cookies aren't overly sweet, making them very snackable for throughout the day. I especially enjoy these cookies with a cup of tea in the afternoon.

1 tbsp (4 g) lemon zest (approximately 1 lemon)

1 cup (200 g) white sugar

½ cup (120 g) butter, softened

1 tsp vanilla extract

1 egg

1 tbsp (15 ml) fresh lemon juice

1½ cups (188 g) all-purpose flour

2 tbsp (16 g) cornstarch

2 tbsp (9 g) poppy seeds

¼ tsp baking powder

⅛ tsp baking soda

¼ tsp kosher salt

Preheat the oven to 325°F (163°C). Line a baking sheet with parchment paper or a silicone mat.

Combine the lemon zest and sugar in a large bowl. Rub with your fingers until evenly distributed. Add the butter. Beat with an electric mixer for about 2 minutes, or until light and fluffy. Add the vanilla, egg, and lemon juice. Beat until combined.

Add the flour, cornstarch, poppy seeds, baking powder, baking soda, and salt. Beat until they are just combined. Use a #40 (2-tablespoon [30-g]) cookie scoop to portion the dough onto the prepared sheet. Roll into balls with your hands.

Bake for 9 to 10 minutes, or until the cookies are puffy and slightly cracked. Remove from the oven before the cookies brown. Let rest for a minute or two before transferring to a wire rack. Store in an airtight container when completely cooled.

Baker's Note: Combining the lemon zest with the sugar and rubbing it with your fingers for just a minute helps distribute the zest throughout your recipe without forming any clumps.

CARAMEL-PRETZEL COOKIES

Yield:
20–24
(4" [10-cm])
cookies

These salty, sweet, chewy, crunchy cookies are filled with cornflakes and pretzels, and generously sprinkled with chewy caramel bits. I was in a cookie-making mood a while back and had already started stirring a batch of cookies together when I discovered that I was out of chocolate chips! (How could that even happen?) I scrounged through the pantry and decided to work with what I had on hand. Lo and behold, I've found my cookie nirvana.

1 cup (200 g) light brown sugar

½ cup (120 g) butter, melted

1 egg

2 tsp (10 ml) vanilla extract

1½ cups (188 g) all-purpose flour

½ tsp baking soda

¼ tsp kosher salt

⅔ cup (80 g) pretzel sticks or twists, roughly chopped (see Baker's Notes)

1 cup (25 g) cornflakes

½ cup (84 g) caramel bits

Preheat the oven to 325°F (163°C). Line a baking sheet with parchment paper or a silicone mat.

Combine the sugar and butter in a large bowl, and beat until smooth. Add the egg and vanilla and beat to combine. Add the flour, baking soda, and salt. Stir again to combine.

Add the pretzels, cornflakes, and caramel bits to the dough. Stir to mix everything throughout the dough. Use a #40 (2-tablespoon [30-g]) cookie scoop to portion onto the prepared baking sheet. Roll into balls. Leave 2 inches (5 cm) between each cookie.

Bake for 12 to 14 minutes. Remove from the oven before the edges of the cookies have browned. The cookies should be puffy and cracked across the top. They will settle as they cool. Allow the cookies to cool for 1 to 2 minutes on the baking sheet and then remove to a wire rack. When the cookies have completely cooled, store in an airtight container.

Baker's Notes: I use straight pretzel sticks for this recipe. Simply chop or break them into thirds. Tiny twist pretzels will work as well; just roughly chop them into bite-size pieces.

Do not refrigerate this dough before baking. The dough is very thick, and it will be rock-firm once cold. If you do need to chill the dough before baking all the cookies, let it come to room temperature again before baking.

SALTED CHOCOLATE CHIP PUDDING COOKIES

Yield:
12–14
(3" [8-cm])
cookies

The magic of a classic pudding cookie is in how chewy the cookies are when they're warm from the oven, and how wonderfully chewy the cookies *still* are three to four days later. That "magic" is usually accomplished with a package of pudding mix.

My original name for these cookies was "Salted Chocolate Chip Pudding Cookies (Without the Pudding Mix!)," but it was a bit much for the title. In lieu of that pudding mix, I've added a spoonful of cornstarch, a little extra sugar, and an extra splash of vanilla. As a result, you get those same fantastic pudding cookies from scratch, without that package of pudding mix.

Feel free to skip the salt on these cookies, if that isn't your thing. But if you haven't yet tried a salted chocolate chip cookie, you are missing out. Try sprinkling salt on just one cookie to try it. You might wind up loving the salted cookies every bit as much as we do.

6 tbsp (84 g) butter, softened

⅓ cup (67 g) light brown sugar

⅓ cup (67 g) white sugar

1 egg

2 tsp (10 ml) vanilla extract

1 cup plus 2 tbsp (140 g) all-purpose flour

1½ tbsp (12 g) cornstarch

½ tsp baking soda

1 cup (168 g) semi-sweet chocolate chips

Sea salt flakes, such as Maldon salt (optional)

Preheat the oven to 350°F (177°C). Line a baking sheet with parchment paper or a silicone mat.

In a large bowl, cream together the butter, brown sugar, and white sugar until light and fluffy. Add the egg and vanilla and beat until smooth. Slowly add in the flour, cornstarch, and baking soda, making sure it is well incorporated. Add the chocolate chips and stir to mix throughout the dough.

Scoop out 2-tablespoon (30-g) portions and roll into balls. Place each ball on the prepared baking sheet. Bake for 11 to 12 minutes. Remove from the oven when the cookies are puffy and barely cooked through—do not let them brown. The cookies should be round and pillow-like (and not browned at all) when they're ready to come out of the oven.

Sprinkle lightly with the salt, if using, as soon as they're out of the oven. Let the cookies cool for 1 minute on the tray and then transfer to a wire rack. As they cool, they will settle into the dips and ridges that are pictured here. Store the completely cool cookies in an airtight container for up to one week.

Baker's Notes: Feel free to swap the chocolate chips with the add-ins of your choice equaling 1 cup (168 g) total.

Take care not to overcook these cookies. For a perfectly chewy pudding cookie, you want to remove them from the oven when they're puffy and not at all browned, and then let them cool on a wire rack.

You do not like them. So you say.

Try them! Try them! And you may.

COCONUT-LIME OATMEAL COOKIES

Yield:
20 (3" [8-cm])
cookies

Soft, chewy oatmeal cookies that are filled with coconut make a great treat for any occasion. If you have a coconut lover in your life, these cookies need to be made sooner rather than later. While the lime glaze is truly perfect on the cookies, it isn't required. The cookies are great on their own as well.

FOR THE COOKIES
½ cup (100 g) light brown sugar

¼ cup (50 g) white sugar

1 tbsp (4 g) finely grated lime zest (approximately 1 lime)

½ cup (120 g) butter, softened

1 egg

1 tsp vanilla extract

1 tbsp (15 ml) fresh lime juice

1¼ cups (156 g) all-purpose flour

¾ cup (60 g) old-fashioned rolled oats

½ tsp baking soda

¼ tsp kosher salt

1 cup (93 g) shredded sweetened coconut

FOR THE GLAZE
1 cup (100 g) powdered sugar

2–3 tbsp (30–45 ml) fresh lime juice

½ cup (47 g) shredded sweetened coconut

Preheat the oven to 325°F (163°C). Line a baking sheet with parchment paper or a silicone mat.

To make the cookies, place the brown sugar, white sugar, and lime zest in a large bowl. Rub with your fingers until evenly distributed. Add the butter and beat until smooth. Add the egg, vanilla, and lime juice and beat. Add the flour, oats, baking soda, and salt. Stir to combine. Add the coconut and stir to combine.

Use a #40 (2-tablespoon [30-g]) cookie scoop to portion the dough onto the prepared baking sheet. Bake for 12 to 14 minutes. Remove from the oven and let them cool for 1 minute on the baking sheet. Transfer to a wire rack to cool completely.

To make the glaze, place the powdered sugar in a small bowl and add the lime juice. Whisk until smooth. Drizzle the glaze over the cooled cookies and sprinkle with the coconut.

Baker's Note: Combining the lime zest with the sugar and rubbing it with your fingers for just a minute helps distribute the zest throughout your recipe without forming any clumps.

CRISPY PEANUT BUTTER COOKIES

Yield: 14–16 (4" [10-cm]) cookies	This is the cookie for the peanut butter purist. Feel free to add chocolate chips or nuts, if you're so inclined, but on its own, this is the cookie for any peanut butter lover. That sprinkling of raw sugar on the outside of the cookie gives it extra crunch alongside that chewy center.

½ cup (120 g) butter, softened

1 cup (200 g) light brown sugar

1 egg

2 tsp (10 ml) vanilla extract

¾ cup (192 g) creamy peanut butter

1 cup (125 g) all-purpose flour

1 tsp baking powder

¼ tsp baking soda

¼ tsp kosher salt

¼ cup (50 g) raw sugar

Preheat the oven to 350°F (177°C). Line a baking sheet with parchment paper or a silicone mat.

In a large bowl, beat the butter and the brown sugar for 2 to 3 minutes, or until fluffy. Add the egg and vanilla and beat until light and fluffy. Add the peanut butter and beat until just combined. Add the flour, baking powder, baking soda, and salt. Mix until just combined.

Place the raw sugar in a shallow bowl. Use a #20 (3-tablespoon [45-g]) cookie scoop to portion the dough into rough ball shapes. Dip the top of each ball into the raw sugar and coat well.

Place the balls on the baking sheet at least 2 inches (5 cm) apart—no more than 6 cookies will fit on a baking sheet. Press down lightly on each ball with a spatula to flatten into a thick disk. Bake for 14 minutes, or until the cookies are lightly brown and cracked on top. They should still be soft, but they will firm up as they cool. Let them cool on the pan for 1 minute before transferring to a wire cooling rack. Let them cool completely before transferring to an airtight container.

Baker's Notes: The key to the crispy edges and chewy center is the extra-large cookie. A generous 3 tablespoons (45 g) of dough goes into each cookie, and it makes a difference in the results. I tried making them smaller, and while tasty, you'll miss the chewy center when you do that.

Make your life easier when measuring peanut butter by greasing the measuring cups with butter (or spraying with nonstick spray) before measuring. The peanut butter will slide right out.

The raw sugar in this recipe adds an extra bit of crunch (that I love), but feel free to use white sugar if that is what you have on hand. Both sugars will work nicely for these cookies.

LITTLE BIT SALTY, LITTLE BIT SWEET SKILLET COOKIES

Yield:
2 (5" [13-cm]) cookies

Salty and sweet treats are taken to a new level when you add in crisp cookie edges, crunchy pretzels, potato chips, pecans, chewy coconut, oats, and gooey chocolate chips.

Anything goes with the add-ins for these cookies. You simply need a total of 1 cup (168 g) of add-in ingredients. The list included with this recipe is my current favorite combination, and I've been making these on repeat for late-night treats.

While typically a skillet cookie is served warm and topped with a scoop of ice cream, this one is such a great combination of textures and flavors that I rarely bother with the ice cream. It's pretty awesome both with ice cream and without.

¼ cup (60 g) butter, melted, plus more for greasing

¼ cup (50 g) light brown sugar

1 egg yolk

½ tsp vanilla extract

⅓ cup (41 g) all-purpose flour

¼ cup (20 g) old-fashioned rolled oats

⅛ tsp baking soda

⅛ tsp kosher salt

2 tbsp (14 g) chopped pecans

2 tbsp (11 g) shredded sweetened coconut

¼ cup (42 g) dark chocolate chips

¼ cup (30 g) roughly chopped pretzels

¼ cup (25 g) broken potato chips with ridges

Preheat the oven to 325°F (163°C). Place 2 (5-inch [13-cm]) pie plates, skillets, or ramekins on a baking tray and lightly grease with butter.

Combine the sugar and the butter in a large bowl. Stir to combine. Add the egg yolk and vanilla and stir. Add the flour, oats, baking soda, and salt. Stir to combine.

Add the pecans, coconut, chocolate chips, pretzels, and potato chips. Stir to mix throughout the dough. Divide the dough between the prepared dishes. Press lightly to spread across each dish.

Bake for 11 to 13 minutes and remove from the oven before the edges of the cookies have browned. The cookies should be puffy and cracked across the top. Let them cool for 2 to 3 minutes before serving.

Baker's Notes: Watch closely as you make these for the first time. Depending on the type of dish or skillet you use, the bake time can vary from 8 to 16 minutes. If they overcook, your dessert will still be delicious, but you'll miss out on the melting gooey aspect of the skillet cookie.

This can also be made in 4 ramekins (3 to 4 ounces [90 to 120 ml]) and baked for 7 to 9 minutes. Or use one 8-inch (20-cm) skillet and bake for 12 to 16 minutes.

FAVORITE OATMEAL RAISIN COOKIES

Yield:
12–14
(4–5"
[10–13-cm])
cookies

Much like chocolate chip cookies, everyone has their own opinion on the perfect oatmeal raisin cookie. For me, this is it: soft, chewy, sweet, and absolutely filled with juicy raisins.

Oatmeal raisin cookies have been a weakness of mine for as long as I can remember. There's just something about the combination of chewy oats, brown sugar, and butter. I really don't ask for much more in an oatmeal cookie.

½ cup (120 g) butter, softened

¾ cup (150 g) light brown sugar

1 egg

1 tsp vanilla extract

1½ cups (120 g) old-fashioned rolled oats

⅔ cup (83 g) all-purpose flour

½ tsp baking soda

¼ tsp kosher salt

½ tsp cinnamon

1 cup (120 g) raisins

Preheat the oven to 350°F (177°C). Line a baking sheet with parchment paper or a silicone mat.

In a large bowl, beat the butter until smooth. Add the sugar and beat for 3 to 4 minutes, or until the mixture is light and fluffy. Add the egg and vanilla and beat until smooth. Add the oats, flour, baking soda, salt, and cinnamon. Stir until fully combined. Add the raisins and stir. Use a #20 (3-tablespoon [45-g]) cookie scoop to drop the dough onto the prepared baking sheet.

Bake for 10 to 11 minutes and remove from the oven before the cookies are browned and when they still look soft, slightly puffy, and cracked—but not wet in the center. Let the cookies cool on the tray for at least 3 to 5 minutes. This will allow them to finish baking from the residual heat on the tray, without overcooking. Transfer to a cooling rack and then store in an airtight container.

CRANBERRY-LEMON SCONE COOKIES

Yield: 12–18 (3" [8-cm]) cookies	Lemon and cranberries are a perfect match, and these tender scones show that off to perfection. These cookies are sophisticated enough to serve to company when you want to impress, but homey, simple, and comforting enough to make just because you want them.

FOR THE COOKIES
1 cup (125 g) all-purpose flour
1 tsp baking powder
¼ tsp kosher salt
⅓ cup (65 g) white sugar
½ cup (120 g) cold butter
3 tbsp (45 ml) fresh lemon juice (see Baker's Notes)
2 tsp (3 g) finely grated lemon zest
1 tsp vanilla extract
1 tbsp (15 ml) milk, plus more if needed
⅓ cup (60 g) dried cranberries or craisins

FOR THE GLAZE
1 cup (100 g) powdered sugar
1–2 tbsp (15–30 ml) lemon juice
Milk, for thinning (optional)

Preheat the oven to 325°F (163°C). Line a baking sheet with parchment paper.

To make the cookies, combine the flour, baking powder, salt, and white sugar in a medium bowl. Stir with a fork to combine. Grate the cold butter and add the butter shreds to the flour mixture. Use a fork to mix the butter into the flour until it's evenly dispersed and approximately pea-sized.

In a medium bowl, stir together lemon juice, lemon zest, vanilla, and the milk. Add the liquids to the flour mixture and stir until a loose, dry dough forms. Add additional milk, only if needed. Gently fold in the cranberries.

Use a #40 (2-tablespoon [30-g]) cookie scoop to portion 12 to 18 balls of dough onto the prepared baking sheet. Press the cookies together with your hands if the dough is crumbling. Bake for 16 to 20 minutes and remove from the oven when barely browned on the bottom, taking care not to brown the tops of the cookies. Transfer the cookies to a wire rack.

To make the glaze, combine the powdered sugar and 1 tablespoon (15 ml) of lemon juice in a small bowl. Whisk until smooth. Add more lemon juice or milk, just a few drops at a time, as needed to thin the glaze. Drizzle the glaze over the cooled cookies and let them cool completely. Store in a loosely covered container.

Baker's Notes: Measure the lemon juice in this recipe carefully, as too much or too little juice will noticeably affect the results. The humidity where you live will affect how much milk is needed in this recipe. I've found that sometimes 1 tablespoon (15 ml) is enough and other times more is needed to make the dough come together. It should be somewhat dry and loose (similar to biscuit dough), and you should be able to press it together with your hands.

The cookies will not spread, so feel free to bake them all on the same baking sheet.

ALMOND LOVERS' CRINKLE COOKIES

Yield:
12–14
(4" [10-cm])
cookies

Crisp on the outside and chewy inside, this cookie is a hit with almond lovers every time I make them. These light cookies are perfect with a cup of tea or coffee. It's one of my personal favorites, and I don't think it's possible to eat just one.

½ cup (120 g) butter, softened

1 cup (200 g) white sugar

½ tsp almond extract

1 egg

1½ cups (188 g) all-purpose flour

¼ tsp baking powder

⅛ tsp baking soda

¼ tsp kosher salt

½ cup (50 g) sliced almonds

Preheat the oven to 350°F (177°C). Line a baking sheet with parchment paper or a silicone mat.

In a large bowl, cream the butter and sugar together until light and fluffy. Add the almond extract and egg. Beat until well combined. Add the flour, baking powder, baking soda, and salt. Stir until they are just combined.

Place the almonds in a small bowl. Use a #40 (2-tablespoon [30-g]) cookie scoop to portion the cookie dough onto the baking sheet. Roll each portion into a ball between your hands, press half of the cookie dough lightly in the almonds, and place almond side up on the prepared baking sheet.

Bake for 11 to 12 minutes, or just until the bottoms of the cookies begin to brown and the cookies are no longer shiny. Remove from the oven and let them rest for a minute or two before transferring to a wire rack. Store in an airtight container when completely cooled.

TRIPLE CHOCOLATE BUTTERSCOTCH SKILLET COOKIE

Yield:
1 (8–10"
[20–25-cm])
cookie

Skillet cookies have a loyal fan base everywhere, and with a scoop of ice cream melting on top, there aren't many desserts that are more popular with my boys. The beauty of a skillet cookie is that gooey center, so take care not to overbake.

A word of caution on the wait time after this comes out of the oven: it will be screaming hot. It's tempting to dig right in on that soft cookie, but give it a few moments to cool just a bit before topping with ice cream and grabbing a spoon.

½ cup (100 g) light brown sugar

¼ cup (60 g) butter, melted

1 egg

1 tsp vanilla extract

1 cup (125 g) all-purpose flour

¼ tsp baking soda

¼ tsp kosher salt

¼ cup (42 g) white chocolate chips

¼ cup (42 g) milk or dark chocolate chips

¼ cup (42 g) semi-sweet chocolate chunks

¼ cup (42 g) butterscotch chips

Sea salt flakes, such as Maldon salt (optional)

Ice cream (optional)

Perfect-Every-Time Hot Fudge (page 156) (optional)

Preheat the oven to 325°F (163°C).

Place the sugar in a large bowl. Add the melted butter and stir until smooth. Add the egg and vanilla and stir. Add the flour, baking soda, and salt to the wet ingredients. Stir to combine. Add the white and milk chocolate chips, chocolate chunks, and butterscotch chips. Stir well to make sure they are evenly distributed.

Press the dough into a lightly greased 10-inch (25-cm) skillet or an 8-inch (20-cm) baking dish. Bake for 14 to 16 minutes, or until the top is puffed up and no longer wet. The cookie should be lightly browned, puffy, and slightly cracked. Remove from the oven. Let it cool for 2 to 3 minutes before topping with the sea salt flakes, ice cream, and/or hot fudge sauce, if desired.

CRANBERRY–WHITE CHOCOLATE COOKIES

Yield:
18 (3" [7.6-cm])
cookies

These are soft and chewy cookies generously filled with dried cranberries and white chocolate. If white chocolate isn't your thing, these are also delicious with dark or semi-sweet chocolate. I like to divide the cookie dough in half before adding the chocolate and then add dark chocolate to one half and white chocolate to the other half.

6 tbsp (84 g) butter, softened

⅓ cup (67 g) light brown sugar

⅓ cup (67 g) white sugar

1 egg

2 tsp (10 ml) vanilla extract

1 tbsp (4 g) orange zest (approximately 1 large orange)

1 cup plus 2 tbsp (140 g) all-purpose flour

2 tbsp (16 g) cornstarch

½ tsp baking soda

¾ tsp cinnamon

1 cup (120 g) dried cranberries or craisins

1 cup (168 g) white chocolate chips

Preheat the oven to 350°F (177°C). Line a baking sheet with parchment paper or a silicone mat.

In a large bowl, cream together the butter, brown sugar, and white sugar until light and fluffy. Add the egg, vanilla, and orange zest and beat until smooth.

Add the flour, cornstarch, baking soda, and cinnamon, making sure it is well incorporated. Add the cranberries and white chocolate chips and stir to mix throughout the dough.

Use a #40 (2-tablespoon [30-g]) cookie scoop to portion the dough into balls. Place them onto the prepared baking sheet. Bake for 9 to 11 minutes. Remove from the oven when they're puffy and barely cooked through—do not let them brown. The cookies should be round and pillowy (and not browned at all) when they're ready to come out of the oven.

Let them cool for 1 minute on the tray and then transfer to a wire rack. They will settle into the dips and ridges that are pictured here as they cool. Store the completely cooled cookies in an airtight container.

M&M'S TREASURE COOKIES

<table>
<tr><td>Yield:
18 (3" [8-cm])
cookies</td><td>Traditionally, treasure cookie recipes have all sorts of fun ingredients tucked into them and get a little something extra from crushed graham crackers. I've found that we prefer the tiny bit of crunch that a handful of cornflakes gives these cookies. This is a great recipe to play with and make your own.</td></tr>
</table>

6 tbsp (90 g) butter, softened

⅔ cup (135 g) light brown sugar

1 egg

1½ tsp (7 ml) vanilla extract

1 cup (125 g) all-purpose flour

½ tsp baking soda

1 cup (25 g) cornflakes

½ cup (84 g) semi-sweet chocolate chips

¾ cup (126 g) M&M's candies

Preheat the oven to 350°F (177°C). Line a baking sheet with parchment paper or a silicone mat.

In a large bowl, cream together the butter and brown sugar until light and fluffy. Add the egg and vanilla and beat until smooth. Slowly add in the flour and baking soda, making sure they are well incorporated. Add the cornflakes, chocolate chips, and M&M's. Stir to mix throughout the dough.

Use a #40 (2-tablespoon [30-g]) cookie scoop to portion the dough into balls. Bake on the prepared baking sheet for 13 to 14 minutes. Remove from the oven when the cookies are puffy and barely cooked through—do not let them brown. The cookies should be round and pillow-like (and not browned at all) when they're ready to come out of the oven. Let them cool for 1 minute on the tray and then transfer to a wire rack. They will settle into dips and ridges as they cool. Store completely cool cookies in an airtight container.

Baker's Note: Any combination of chocolate chips, chopped nuts, and M&M's candies will work in these cookies. Just make sure you add in a total amount of 1¼ cups (210 g) to substitute for the amounts listed above.

NUT LOVERS' OATMEAL COOKIES

Yield:
18 (3" [8-cm])
cookies

These chewy, bakery-style cookies have crisp edges and a soft center. They're filled with an assortment of chewy nuts, making them a salty-sweet cookie that I can't resist.

It amazes me that I feel no need to add chocolate to these cookies. I imagine they would be fantastic with a handful of chocolate chips thrown into the mix, but the chocolate is not required. Every single person who has tasted these cookies has raved about how awesome they are.

This is the ultimate clean-out-the-pantry cookie for nut lovers. If you're as big a fan of the sweet-and-salty combination as I am, sprinkle the tops of these cookies with a pinch of salt flakes as soon as they come out of the oven.

⅔ cup plus 2 tbsp (160 g) light brown sugar

½ cup (120 g) butter, melted

1 egg

1½ tsp (7 ml) vanilla extract

1 cup (125 g) all-purpose flour

½ cup plus 2 tbsp (50 g) old-fashioned rolled oats

¼ tsp baking soda

¼ tsp kosher salt

¾ cup (84 g) chopped assorted nuts, such as pecans, walnuts, and peanuts

Sea salt flakes, such as Maldon salt (optional)

Preheat the oven to 325°F (163°C). Line a baking sheet with parchment paper or a silicone mat.

Place the sugar in a large bowl. Add the melted butter and beat until smooth. Add the egg and vanilla and beat. Add the flour, oats, baking soda, and salt to the wet ingredients. Stir to combine. Add the nuts and stir well to make sure they are evenly distributed.

Scoop the dough into 1½-inch (4-cm) sized balls and place on the prepared baking sheet. Bake for 14 to 16 minutes. Remove from the oven before the cookies have browned. Let them cool for 1 to 2 minutes on the baking sheet and then transfer to a wire rack.

Baker's Note: I like to use an assortment of nuts when making these cookies. The nuts I use are roasted and salted. Whatever nuts you have on hand will work nicely.

CHOCOLATE MINT COOKIES

Yield:
18 (2–3"
[5–8-cm])
cookies

Tender, melt-in-your-mouth, chocolate mint cookies filled with gooey bites of chocolate have proved absolutely irresistible to everyone we've shared these cookies with. This rich chocolate cookie almost begs for a glass of milk or a scoop of ice cream alongside it.

½ cup (120 g) butter, softened

½ cup (100 g) light brown sugar

⅓ cup (67 g) white sugar

1 egg

1 tsp vanilla extract

½ tsp peppermint extract

1 cup (125 g) all-purpose flour

1 tbsp (8 g) cornstarch

½ cup (43 g) cocoa powder

½ tsp baking powder

¼ tsp baking soda

¼ tsp kosher salt

½ cup (84 g) semi-sweet chocolate chips

½ cup (84 g) chopped chocolate mint candies, such as Andes mints (approximately 14 mints)

Preheat the oven to 350°F (177°C). Line a baking sheet with parchment paper or a silicone mat.

In a bowl, beat the butter, brown sugar, and white sugar for 2 minutes, or until smooth. Add the egg, vanilla, and peppermint extract. Beat until smooth. Add the flour, cornstarch, cocoa powder, baking powder, baking soda, and salt. Beat until just combined. Stir in the chocolate chips and chocolate mints.

Use a #40 (2-tablespoon [30-g]) cookie scoop to portion the dough onto the prepared baking sheet, leaving at least 2 inches (5 cm) between the cookies. Bake the cookies for 7 to 8 minutes, or until the cookies have puffed up and begun to crack. Allow the cookies to cool on the baking sheet for 2 minutes before transferring to a wire rack to cool completely.

Baker's Notes: Be very careful when adding the peppermint extract. Peppermint is a significantly stronger extract than vanilla extract. Too much peppermint will ruin the flavor and might cause the cookies to taste a bit like toothpaste.

If chocolate mints are not available, you'll want to use a milk- or dark-chocolate candy with the flavor of mint added.

Take care not to overbake these cookies—this is a tender and gooey chocolate cookie that will dry out if overbaked.

CREAM CHEESE–PECAN COOKIES

<table>
<tr><td>Yield:
12 (2–3"
[5–7.6-cm])
cookies</td><td>This is a buttery, melt-in-your-mouth cookie that is absolutely loaded with bits of pecans. This may not be the prettiest cookie you'll ever make, but if you love pecans, you will truly adore this cookie. This is my husband's favorite cookie in this book.

Perfect as an afternoon snack with tea or coffee, this isn't an overly sweet cookie. If I have these in the house, the odds are high that I will enjoy a couple with my morning coffee, too.</td></tr>
</table>

¼ cup (60 g) butter, softened

½ cup (100 g) light brown sugar

4 oz (113 g) cream cheese, softened

1 tsp vanilla extract

½ cup (62 g) all-purpose flour

1 cup (109 g) finely chopped pecans, plus 2 tbsp (14 g) for topping

Preheat the oven to 350°F (177°C). Line a baking sheet with parchment paper or a silicone mat.

In a large bowl, combine the butter, sugar, cream cheese, and vanilla. Beat with an electric mixer until smooth. Add the flour and 1 cup (109 g) of pecans and beat.

Use a #40 (2-tablespoon [30-g]) cookie scoop to portion the dough onto the prepared baking sheet. These cookies don't spread much at all, so feel free to bake them all on the same sheet. Press each cookie flat to about a ½-inch (1.3-cm) height with the back of a spatula. Top the cookies with the remaining 2 tablespoons (14 g) of pecans.

Bake for approximately 10 to 11 minutes. Remove from the oven before the cookies are browned. Let them cool on the sheet for 1 to 2 minutes, and then remove to a wire cooling rack.

> *Baker's Note:* I typically toss pecan halves in the food processor and whirl them around a couple of times to create the tiny pieces I use in this recipe. However, you can also buy them finely chopped.

OATMEAL PEANUT BUTTER CUP SKILLET COOKIES

Yield:
6 (4" [10-cm]) cookies

Crisp-edged cookies filled with chewy oats and melting chocolate and peanut butter cups are a hit with my crew. My family loves a gooey skillet cookie, but we also tend to be a little territorial when it comes to sharing our desserts. These individual cookies are a super-fun way to make sure we all get our favorite bites in each serving.

These cookies can be made in any small ramekin or baking dish. While the tiny skillets are cute, they are not required for the recipe.

The flavor combination in these skillet cookies is one of my favorites in the book. I often make this as a bar cookie as well. Just follow the directions in the Baker's Note for baking in an 8-inch (20-cm) sqaure pan and then let it cool completely before slicing into bars.

6 tbsp (84 g) butter, softened

⅔ cup (135 g) light brown sugar

1 egg

1 tsp vanilla extract

1¼ cups (100 g) old-fashioned rolled oats

½ cup (62 g) all-purpose flour

½ tsp baking soda

¼ tsp kosher salt

¼ cup (42 g) peanut butter chips

¼ cup (42 g) semi-sweet chocolate chips

6–12 miniature peanut butter cups

Ice cream, for serving (optional)

Preheat the oven to 350°F (177°C). Grease 6 ramekins (3 to 4 ounces [90 to 120 ml]) or 6 skillets (4 inches [10 cm]).

In a large bowl, add the butter and sugar. Stir to mix well. Add the egg and vanilla and stir until smooth. Add the oats, flour, baking soda, and salt. Stir until fully combined. Stir in the peanut butter chips and chocolate chips.

Divide the batter into the prepared dishes and spread evenly across each dish. Press 1 to 2 peanut butter cups into the top of each cookie.

Bake for 8 to 12 minutes and remove from the oven when the cookies are lightly browned and look soft, slightly puffy, and cracked, but not wet in the center. Let them cool for 2 to 3 minutes before serving. Top with ice cream, if desired.

Baker's Notes: If you prefer one big skillet cookie or bars, this can be baked in a 10-inch (25-cm) skillet or an 8-inch (20-cm) square baking dish. Watch the baking time and add 3 to 6 minutes to the recommended baking time, as needed.

Make your life easier when measuring peanut butter by greasing the measuring cups with butter (or spray with nonstick spray) before measuring. The peanut butter will slide right out.

This recipe calls for the tiny peanut butter cups that are sold unwrapped in a bag, not the individually wrapped bite-size variety.

ALMOND JOY COOKIES

Yield:	These cookies are absolutely loaded with coconut, chocolate, and almonds. They're soft and chewy cookies with crisp edges and gooey chocolate inside. I'm a coconut lover for life and these cookies are some of my favorites.
18 (3" [8-cm]) cookies	

6 tbsp (84 g) butter, softened

⅓ cup (67 g) light brown sugar

⅓ cup (67 g) white sugar

1 egg

½ tsp coconut extract

¼ tsp almond extract

1 cup plus 2 tbsp (140 g) all-purpose flour

2 tbsp (16 g) cornstarch

½ tsp baking soda

¼ tsp kosher salt

1 cup (93 g) shredded sweetened coconut

1 cup (168 g) dark chocolate chips

½ cup (50 g) sliced almonds

Preheat the oven to 350°F (177°C). Line a baking sheet with parchment paper or a silicone mat.

Combine the butter, brown sugar, and white sugar in a large bowl. Beat with an electric mixer until light and fluffy. Add the egg, coconut extract, and almond extract. Beat until smooth. Add the flour, cornstarch, baking soda, and salt. Beat to mix well. Add the coconut, chocolate chips, and almonds. Stir to mix throughout the dough.

Use a #40 (2-tablespoon [30-g]) cookie scoop to portion the dough into balls on the prepared baking sheet. Bake for 9 to 11 minutes. Remove from the oven when the cookies are puffy and barely cooked through—do not let them brown. The cookies should be round and pillow-like (and not browned at all) when they're ready to come out of the oven. Let them cool for 1 minute on the tray and then transfer to a wire rack. They will settle as they cool. Store the completely cooled cookies in an airtight container.

CRISPY CHOCOLATE-TOFFEE COOKIES

Yield:
24–28
(3" [8-cm])
cookies

These thin and crispy-edged chocolate cookies are filled with chewy toffee bits and gooey chocolate. These cookies just beg for a glass of milk or a bowl of ice cream. This is a sturdy cookie that keeps nicely. It is perfect for tucking into lunches.

¼ cup (60 g) butter, softened

½ cup (100 g) light brown sugar

⅓ cup (65 g) white sugar

1 egg

1 tsp vanilla extract

⅔ cup (83 g) all-purpose flour

⅓ cup (29 g) cocoa powder

¼ tsp kosher salt

½ tsp baking soda

½ cup (84 g) dark or semi-sweet chocolate chips

½ cup (84 g) toffee bits

Preheat the oven to 325°F (163°C). Line a baking sheet with parchment paper or a silicone mat.

In a bowl, beat the butter, brown sugar, and white sugar for 2 to 3 minutes, or until smooth. Add the egg and vanilla and beat. Add the flour, cocoa powder, salt, and baking soda to the wet ingredients and beat until just combined. Stir in the chocolate chips and toffee bits.

Use a #50 (1-tablespoon [15-g]) cookie scoop to portion the dough onto the prepared baking sheet, leaving at least 2 inches (5 cm) between the cookies. (They will spread a lot.) Bake the cookies for 8 minutes, or until they begin to puff up and crisp on the edges. The cookies should be dry on top but still very soft when you remove them from the oven. Allow the cookies to cool on the baking sheet for at least 5 minutes before transferring them to a wire rack to cool completely.

MAPLE-NUT SCONE COOKIES

Yield:
12–18
(3" [8-cm])
cookies

These chewy maple cookies are generously studded with pecans and drizzled with a maple frosting. These are THE cookies with all the texture of a soft, chewy scone and a perfect balance of pecans and maple. I shared these cookies on my website a couple of years ago, and they continue to be one of my all-time favorite cookie recipes. I couldn't make a dessert book and not include them.

FOR THE COOKIES

1 cup (125 g) all-purpose flour

1 tsp baking powder

¼ tsp kosher salt

⅓ cup (67 g) raw sugar, plus more for topping

¼ cup (60 g) cold butter

⅓ cup (80 ml) plus 1–2 tbsp (15–30 ml) heavy cream (see Baker's Notes)

1 tbsp (15 ml) maple syrup

½ tsp vanilla extract

½ cup (55 g) chopped pecans

FOR THE GLAZE

1 cup (100 g) powdered sugar

3 tbsp (45 ml) maple syrup

1 tsp cream or milk, plus more if needed

¾ tsp vanilla extract

Preheat the oven to 350°F (177°C). Line a large baking sheet with parchment paper.

To make the cookies, combine the flour, baking powder, salt, and raw sugar in a medium bowl. Stir with a fork to combine. Grate the cold butter and add the shreds to the flour mixture. Use a fork to mix the butter into the flour until it's evenly dispersed and approximately pea-sized.

In a medium bowl, stir together ⅓ cup (80 ml) of the heavy cream, the maple syrup, and vanilla. Add the liquids to the flour mixture, and stir until a loose, dry dough forms. Add additional cream only if needed. Gently fold in the pecans. Use a #40 (2-tablespoon [30-g]) cookie scoop to portion 12 to 18 balls of dough onto the prepared baking sheet. Press the cookies together with your hands, if the dough is crumbling. Sprinkle each cookie with raw sugar before baking.

Bake for 18 to 20 minutes and remove the cookies from the oven when they're barely browned on the bottom, taking care not to brown the tops of the cookies. Transfer the cookies to a wire rack.

To make the glaze, combine the powdered sugar, maple syrup, cream, and vanilla in a small bowl. Whisk until smooth. Add more cream or milk, just a few drops at a time, as needed to thin the glaze. Drizzle the glaze over the cooled cookies.

Baker's Notes: The humidity where you live will affect how much cream is needed in this recipe. I've found that sometimes ⅓ cup (80 ml) is enough and other times additional liquid is needed to make the dough come together. It should be somewhat dry and loose (similar to biscuit dough) and you should be able to press it together with your hands.

The cookies will not spread, so feel free to bake them all on the same baking sheet.

The raw sugar in this recipe provides a distinct flavor and texture. Plain white sugar will not yield the same results.

PRETZEL PEANUT BUTTER CUP COOKIES

<table>
<tr><td>

Yield:
24 (3–4"
[7.6–10-cm])
cookies

</td><td>

Chewy cookies filled with tiny peanut butter cups and salty pretzels are a kid favorite in my house. They can't get enough of these cookies. In case you haven't yet noticed, salty-sweet pairings are my favorite thing ever when it comes to snacks and desserts. There's just something extra special and unexpected about that hint of salt in each sweet bite.

Don't let the oats in this recipe deter you from trying them. There is barely a hint of oatmeal flavor, and it provides a chewy texture that can't be beat.

</td></tr>
</table>

1¾ cups (350 g) light brown sugar

½ cup (120 g) butter, melted

1 egg

2 tsp (10 ml) vanilla extract

1¼ cups (156 g) all-purpose flour

¾ cup (60 g) old-fashioned rolled oats

¼ tsp baking soda

¼ tsp kosher salt

⅔ cup (80 g) broken pretzel sticks

1 cup (168 g) mini peanut butter cups, divided

Preheat the oven to 325°F (163°C). Line a baking sheet with parchment paper or a silicone mat.

Place the sugar in a large bowl. Add the hot, melted butter and beat until smooth. Add the egg and vanilla and beat. Add the flour, oats, baking soda, and salt to the wet ingredients. Stir to combine. Add the pretzels and ⅔ cup (112 g) of the peanut butter cups. Stir well to make sure they are evenly distributed. Don't worry if the cups break in the dough.

Use a #40 (2-tablespoon [30-g]) cookie scoop to portion the dough into slightly-smaller-than-golf-ball-sized rounds and place on the prepared baking sheet. Press a peanut butter cup into the top of each ball of cookie dough. Bake for 13 to 14 minutes. Remove from the oven and let them cool for 1 to 2 minutes on the baking sheet. Transfer the cookies to a wire rack and cool completely before storing in an airtight container.

Baker's Notes: Be careful to break or chop, but not crush, the pretzels. You want small bite-size pieces of pretzel for each cookie, not pretzel dust.

This recipe calls for the tiny peanut butter cups that are sold unwrapped in a bag, not the individually wrapped bite-size variety.

PISTACHIO–CHOCOLATE CHUNK COOKIES

Yield:
18 small
(3" [8-cm])
cookies

These are chewy cookies filled with chocolate chunks and sprinkled throughout with pistachios. The pistachio flavor is not dominant, but it's enough to make you stop and think about what is making them unique. We've also made these cookies with dark chocolate chips, and I enjoy that variation as well. My kids like the recipe best as written below.

⅔ cup (135 g) light brown sugar

½ cup (120 g) butter, melted

1 egg

2 tsp (10 ml) vanilla extract

1 cup (125 g) all-purpose flour

½ cup (40 g) old-fashioned rolled oats

¼ tsp baking soda

¼ tsp kosher salt

¼ cup (28 g) chopped pistachio nuts

¾ cup (126 g) semi-sweet chocolate chunks

Preheat the oven to 325°F (163°C). Line a baking sheet with parchment paper or a silicone mat.

Place the sugar in a large bowl. Add the hot melted butter and beat until smooth. Add the egg and vanilla and beat. Add the flour, oats, baking soda, and salt. Beat to combine. Add the pistachios and chocolate chunks and stir well to make sure they are evenly distributed.

Use a #40 (2-tablespoon [30-g]) cookie scoop to portion the dough and roll the dough into balls. Place on the prepared baking sheet and bake for 12 minutes. Remove from the oven and let the cookies cool for 1 to 2 minutes on the baking sheet and then transfer to a wire rack.

Baker's Note: The pistachios in this recipe should be measured as shelled nuts, not pistachios in the shell. I use salted pistachios, because we enjoy salty-sweet desserts. However, unsalted pistachios will work nicely as well.

Bars: The Ultimate Make-Ahead Dessert

While cookies are fantastic, bars take that deliciousness and add the incredible convenience of being baked all at once in a single pan. Bars are always a crowd-pleaser, and they're an easy way to deliver sophisticated flavors with minimal effort.

Classic dessert flavors get a modern twist in Black Forest Brownies (page 110), Monster Cookie Bars (page 93), Chai Snickerdoodle Bars (page 94), and PB&J Blondies (page 102). Don't forget the decadent Gooey Rocky Road Brownies (page 101) for the kids (and the adults) and the Irish Coffee Bars (page 113) just for adults.

Here are three tips to help make sure your bars come out perfectly every time:

- Create a parchment sling. Before pouring your batter or transferring your dough to the pan, line it with parchment so that the paper extends up beyond the rim of the pan by at least 1 inch (2.5 cm). The benefit to using parchment is that you can lift those overhanging edges and the whole baked good comes easily out of the pan. Plunk it onto a cutting board and you can cut it directly on the parchment paper.

- Work the plan. While recipes are made to be altered (and I'm a huge fan of doing so), try each recipe as written as closely as possible the first time, so you know what the final product is meant to be like. It's absolutely okay to swap certain ingredients in and out of things, but until you've made them in the original form at least once, you may not know which ingredients are integral to the success of the final product.

- Be patient. While it's tempting to cut into those hot brownies or cookie bars, you'll be rewarded for your patience if you let them cool for at least 15 minutes before cutting them. This is because there is carry-over cooking taking place from the heat of the baked goods as they continue to cool. You won't get an accurate idea of the final texture until they're completely cooled to room temperature. And the truth is that they store better if you wait to cut them until they're cool.

Speaking of cutting into your desserts, if you just don't want to wait for things to cool, a cheap plastic knife (the kind you would throw away after a picnic) will cut warm brownies like a dream. That's one of the best tricks I have for slicing warm desserts and not having them fall apart.

MONSTER COOKIE BARS

Yield:
9 bars

Monster cookies have been my family's favorite cookie ever since I was a child. We use Grandma McGinnis's recipe and make a giant batch of the cookies every year for our family's camping trip.

These bars are a nod to Grandma's recipe, with the ease of a bar cookie. Slightly gooier than the cookies and still crisp on top and bottom, this is one of the best bar cookies I've ever tasted.

3 tbsp (45 g) butter, softened

¾ cup (150 g) light brown sugar

⅓ cup (65 g) white sugar

1 egg

1 egg yolk

1 tsp vanilla extract

1 tbsp (15 ml) maple syrup

½ tsp baking soda

⅔ cup (172 g) crunchy peanut butter

2 cups (160 g) old-fashioned rolled oats

⅓–½ cup (56–84 g) semi-sweet chocolate chips

¼–½ cup (42–84 g) M&M's candies for topping

Preheat the oven to 350°F (177°C). Line an 8-inch (20-cm) square pan with parchment paper or grease well with butter.

Combine the butter, brown sugar, and white sugar in a large bowl and beat to combine. Add the egg, egg yolk, vanilla, syrup, and baking soda. Stir in the peanut butter. Add the oats and stir until well combined. Mix in the chocolate chips.

Press the dough into the bottom of the prepared pan. Top with the M&M's and lightly press them into the dough. Bake for 16 to 17 minutes, or until the bars are lightly browned and just past looking wet on top. They will not be firm, but they will set up as they cool. Let it cool completely before slicing. Store in an airtight container.

Baker's Notes: Monster Cookies were gluten free before that was a thing, so these are a terrific flourless option for sharing with friends who avoid gluten. If you're dealing with an allergy, as always, read the labels and be certain your oats and other ingredients are certified gluten free.

Make your life easier when measuring peanut butter by greasing the measuring cups with butter (or spray with nonstick spray) before measuring. The peanut butter will slide right out.

CHAI SNICKERDOODLE BARS

Yield:
8–10 bars

These are tender, melt-in-your-mouth cookie bars with all the chai flavors that we love topped with a generous sprinkling of cinnamon-sugar. I expected this to be a dessert that the adults would enjoy more than the kids, but my younger two boys wound up absolutely loving them. The spices add so much flavor to the bars and no one can eat just one.

FOR THE BARS
½ cup (120 g) butter, softened
1 cup (200 g) white sugar
½ tsp vanilla extract
1 egg
1¾ cups (218 g) all-purpose flour
2 tsp (15 g) baking powder
¼ tsp kosher salt
¼ tsp ground cinnamon
¾ tsp ground ginger
½ tsp ground cardamom
¼ tsp cloves
⅛ tsp very finely ground black pepper

FOR THE TOPPING
1½ tbsp (18 g) sugar
1 tsp ground cinnamon

Preheat the oven to 325°F (163°C). Line a 9 x 13–inch (23 x 33–cm) pan with parchment paper or grease lightly with butter.

To make the bars, combine the butter and sugar in a large bowl. Beat to mix well. Add the vanilla and the egg. Stir until smooth. Add the flour, baking powder, salt, cinnamon, ginger, cardamom, cloves, and pepper. Beat to combine. Press the batter into the prepared pan.

To make the topping, stir together the sugar and cinnamon in a small bowl. Sprinkle the bars generously with the cinnamon-sugar.

Bake for 14 to 16 minutes and remove from the oven when the bars are slightly puffy and no longer wet. Do not let them brown. Let them cool completely before slicing into bars.

BLUEBERRY–CHOCOLATE CHUNK BROWNIES

<table>
<tr><td>Yield:
9–12 servings</td><td>Brownies filled with melting chocolate and bursting blueberries? Yes! You might doubt the awesomeness of these brownies at first glance, but I'm willing to bet you'll be a fan from the first bite. My sister is the person I will forever owe for introducing me to the amazing combination of blueberries and chocolate. I doubted her until I tried it, and then I was hooked. In fact, these brownies have been a huge win with everyone who has tasted them, even the skeptics. These brownies are pretty fantastic on their own or when layered into Blueberry Brownie Trifles (page 182).</td></tr>
</table>

¼ cup (60 g) butter, plus more for pan

1¾ cups (294 g) semi-sweet chocolate chips, divided

½ cup (100 g) light brown sugar

1 tbsp (15 ml) vanilla extract

2 eggs

½ cup (62 g) all-purpose flour

¼ tsp kosher salt

1 cup (148 g) blueberries

Preheat the oven to 325°F (163°C). Grease an 8-inch (20-cm) square pan with butter or line with parchment paper.

Melt the butter in a medium saucepan over medium-high heat. Add 1 cup (168 g) of the chocolate chips and stir until melted. Remove from the heat. Add the brown sugar and vanilla, and stir until smooth.

Whisk in the eggs. Add the flour and salt. Stir until well combined. Stir in the blueberries and the remaining chocolate chips. Pour the brownie batter into the prepared pan. Bake for 28 to 30 minutes, or until a toothpick inserted in the center of the brownies comes out with wet crumbs.

Baker's Notes: These brownies will keep nicely in an airtight container at room temperature for several days. Alternatively, they can be wrapped airtight and frozen for up to three months. Thaw at room temperature before eating.

Frozen blueberries work well in this recipe. The frozen berries can be added to the recipe without thawing.

CRANBERRY-PISTACHIO OATMEAL BARS

Yield: 8–10 bars	These cranberry-pistachio bars are a chewy treat that I cannot resist when they're in my house. They're similar to a soft and chewy granola bar, but so much better. I typically snack on these treats on their own, but they're also delicious with a scoop of ice cream on top.

6 tbsp (90 g) butter, softened, plus more for pan

⅔ cup (135 g) light brown sugar

1 egg

1 tsp vanilla extract

1¼ cups (100 g) old-fashioned rolled oats

½ cup (62 g) all-purpose flour

½ tsp baking soda

¼ tsp kosher salt

⅔ cup (96 g) dried cranberries

½ cup (55 g) roasted unsalted pistachios

Preheat the oven to 350°F (177°C). Grease an 8-inch (20-cm) square pan with butter or line with parchment paper.

Combine the butter and brown sugar in a large bowl and stir to mix well. Add the egg and vanilla and stir until smooth. Add the oats, flour, baking soda, and salt. Stir until fully combined. Add the cranberries and pistachios. Stir to mix throughout. Press the batter into the prepared pan.

Bake for 16 to 18 minutes, or until browned, slightly puffy, and cracked around the edges. Let it cool completely before slicing into bars.

Baker's Notes: Salted pistachios may be substituted for the unsalted nuts listed in this recipe. Be aware that the bars will be a sweet-and-salty combination with that option. It distinctly changes the overall flavor of the bars. They're good both ways, but the unsalted pistachios are my first choice.

The bars will be soft when first baked and will firm up a bit overnight.

GOOEY ROCKY ROAD BROWNIES

<table>
<tr><td>Yield:
12–16 servings</td><td>Gooey fudge brownies are filled with marshmallows and topped with rich chocolate ganache. These are a super-rich treat. Slice them small and enjoy with a glass of milk.</td></tr>
</table>

FOR THE BROWNIES

¼ cup (60 g) butter, plus more for pan

1¾ cups (294 g) semi-sweet chocolate chips, divided

½ cup (100 g) light brown sugar

1 tbsp (15 ml) vanilla extract

2 eggs

½ cup (62 g) all-purpose flour

¼ tsp kosher salt

2½ cups (125 g) miniature marshmallows, divided

FOR THE TOPPING

½ cup (120 ml) heavy cream

½ cup (84 g) semi-sweet chocolate chips

¼ cup (26 g) powdered sugar

3 tbsp (18 g) unsweetened cocoa powder

½ cup (50 g) sliced almonds

Preheat the oven to 325°F (163°C). Grease an 8-inch (20-cm) square pan with butter or line with parchment paper.

To make the brownies, melt the butter in a medium saucepan over medium-high heat. Add 1 cup (168 g) of the chocolate chips and stir until melted. Remove from the heat. Add the brown sugar and vanilla, and stir until smooth. Whisk in the eggs. Add the flour and salt. Stir until well combined. Stir in 2 cups (100 g) of the marshmallows and the remaining ¾ cup (126 g) of chocolate chips.

Pour the brownie batter into the prepared pan and sprinkle with the remaining marshmallows. Bake for 26 to 28 minutes, or until a toothpick inserted in the center of the brownies comes out with wet crumbs.

To make the topping, warm the cream in a medium-size glass bowl in the microwave for 60 to 90 seconds, or until simmering. Add the chocolate chips to the cream and let it sit for 2 minutes. Whisk until the chocolate mixture is smooth and glossy. Add the sugar and cocoa powder and whisk again until completely smooth. Remove the brownies from the oven and pour the frosting over the top. Sprinkle with the almonds. Let the brownies cool completely before slicing into bars.

PB&J BLONDIES

Yield:
9–12 servings

These blondies are perfect with a glass of milk for an afternoon snack or an after-dinner treat. They aren't overly sweet, and they're absolutely loaded with peanut butter flavor. My PB&J-loving youngest son loves them immensely. These bars freeze nicely and reheat beautifully in the microwave.

¼ cup (60 g) butter, softened, plus more for pan

½ cup (129 g) creamy peanut butter

¾ cup (150 g) light brown sugar

2 eggs

2 tsp (10 ml) vanilla extract

¾ cup (93 g) all-purpose flour

¼ tsp baking powder

¼ tsp kosher salt

¾ cup (84 g) chopped peanuts, divided

¼ cup (80 g) strawberry or grape jam

Preheat the oven to 350°F (177°C). Grease an 8-inch (20-cm) baking pan with butter or line with parchment paper.

Combine the peanut butter, butter, brown sugar, eggs, and vanilla in a large bowl. Stir until smooth and creamy. Add the flour, baking powder, and salt and stir to combine. Add ½ cup (55 g) of the chopped peanuts and stir.

Spread the mixture in the prepared baking pan. Drop spoonfuls of jam over the blondies and swirl lightly with a knife. The peanut butter mixture will be thick, but the jam will bake into it nicely. Sprinkle with the remaining peanuts. Bake for 25 to 28 minutes, or until a toothpick inserted comes out mostly clean or with wet crumbs. Let it cool completely before slicing into bars.

Baker's Note: Make your life easier when measuring peanut butter by greasing the measuring cups with butter (or spraying with nonstick spray) before measuring. The peanut butter will slide right out.

WALNUT TOFFEE BARS

Yield:
16–20 bars

These rich, buttery bars are absolutely loaded with toffee flavor and crunchy walnuts. They are a sweet treat, so we like to slice them pretty small. While I absolutely love these bars with walnuts, I realize that not everyone enjoys the sharp flavor of this nut. If walnuts aren't your thing, pecans will work nicely in this recipe.

½ cup (120 g) butter, melted

1 cup (200 g) light brown sugar

1 egg

2 tsp (10 ml) vanilla extract

1 cup (125 g) all-purpose flour

¼ tsp kosher salt

1 cup (109 g) chopped walnuts, divided

1 cup (168 g) toffee bits, divided

Preheat the oven to 350°F (177°C). Line an 8-inch (20-cm) square pan with parchment paper or grease the pan well.

Combine the butter and brown sugar in a large bowl and stir well to combine. Add the egg and vanilla and stir again. Add the flour and salt and stir well. Stir in the walnuts and toffee bits, reserving 2 tablespoons of each (14 g of walnuts and 21 g of toffee bits) for the topping. Scoop into the prepared pan and spread evenly with a spatula. Sprinkle with the reserved nuts and toffee bits.

Bake for 25 to 28 minutes, or until a toothpick inserted comes out mostly clean with moist crumbs. Let the bars cool completely before slicing.

OATMEAL-ALMOND FUDGE BARS

<table>
<tr><td>Yield:
9–12 bars</td><td>Chewy oatmeal and almond bars layered with chocolate fudge are a rich dessert that is also a terrific handheld treat. The bars are sliceable if you let them cool completely, but I often scoop this dessert warm from the oven and then top with vanilla ice cream (page 143). A drizzling of hot fudge (page 156) will take this one right over the top.</td></tr>
</table>

FOR THE COOKIE LAYER
½ cup (100 g) packed light brown sugar

½ cup (120 g) butter, melted

1 large egg

1 tsp vanilla extract

½ tsp almond extract

2 cups (160 g) quick-cooking oatmeal

1¼ cups (156 g) all-purpose flour

½ tsp baking soda

½ tsp salt

½ cup (50 g) sliced almonds

FOR THE FUDGE LAYER
1 cup (168 g) semi-sweet or dark chocolate chips

¼ cup (60 ml) heavy cream

⅛ tsp almond extract

Preheat the oven to 350°F (177°C). Line an 8-inch (20-cm) baking pan with parchment paper.

To make the cookie layer, combine the brown sugar and butter in a large bowl and beat until combined. Add the egg, vanilla, and almond extract and beat to combine. Add the oatmeal, flour, baking soda, and salt. Beat to combine. Stir in the almonds. Scoop about three-quarters of the dough into the prepared pan and press the dough to the edges.

To make the fudge layer, combine the chocolate chips, cream, and almond extract in a small glass bowl or measuring cup. Microwave for 60 seconds, or until the chips are soft. Stir for 1 minute, or until it's smooth and glossy.

Pour the fudge over the dough in the pan. Drop the remaining cookie dough over the fudge layer. Bake the bars for 16 minutes, or until a toothpick inserted into the center comes out with just a few moist crumbs. When completely cooled, remove from the pan and cut into small squares. These will keep well in an airtight container for several days.

Baker's Note: This recipe doubles nicely for a 9 x 13–inch (23 x 33–cm) pan.

GINGER SHORTBREAD BARS

Yield:
18–24 small bars

This is a buttery, melt-in-your-mouth shortbread recipe that we all love so much. This isn't a dry or crumbly shortbread. There's a place for that, but it isn't here. This is tender, soft shortbread, and it's gently adapted from a recipe my Aunt Judy gave me years ago.

If you love ginger, this is the treat for you. This is a terrific make-ahead dessert as the flavor deepens by the second day. The nuts in this recipe are optional, but we enjoy the added flavor they provide.

FOR THE BARS

½ cup (120 g) butter, softened, plus more for pan

1 cup (200 g) white sugar

1 egg

½ tsp vanilla extract

2 cups (250 g) all-purpose flour

1½ tsp (8 g) baking powder

¼ tsp kosher salt

1½ tsp (3 g) ground ginger

1 cup (109 g) chopped pecans or walnuts (optional)

FOR THE TOPPING

1 cup (100 g) powdered sugar

1 tsp ground ginger

1–2 tbsp (15–30 ml) water or milk

Preheat the oven to 325°F (163°C). Lightly grease a 9 x 13–inch (23 x 33–cm) pan with butter or line with parchment paper.

To make the bars, cream together the butter and white sugar in a large bowl. Add the egg and the vanilla and mix until light and fluffy. Add the flour, baking powder, salt, and ginger and mix until combined. Stir in the nuts, if desired. Transfer the crumbly dough to the prepared pan. Press it firmly with your hands or with a pastry roller to create an even layer and smooth the top of the dough.

Bake for 14 minutes, or until just barely beginning to harden around the edges. Do not allow the bars to brown at all. If they brown, they will be much more crunchy than desired. The goal is a very soft shortbread texture. Let cool in the pan for 15 minutes and then cut into bars. If they are too soft to cut, let them cool for a few more minutes. Remove them carefully to a wire rack to cool completely.

To make the topping, whisk together the powdered sugar, ground ginger, and 1 tablespoon (15 ml) of the water or milk in a medium bowl. Stir with a spoon or whisk and add more water or milk, a few drops at a time, until the glaze is smooth and still slightly thick. It should pour smoothly off the spoon. Drizzle the glaze over the bars and let set completely before storing in an airtight container.

Variation: Skip the ground ginger and add 1 teaspoon of almond extract to the bars and ½ teaspoon of almond extract to the glaze.

Baker's Notes: Baking the shortbread in a pan and then slicing it into bars makes this a very easy dessert. This recipe doubles perfectly and fills a large baking sheet.

Placing a sheet of parchment on top of the dough will make it easier to press/roll the dough and spread it across the pan. Remove the parchment from on top of the bars before baking.

BLACK FOREST BROWNIES

Yield:
12–16 servings

Black Forest Brownies are extra gooey fudge brownies filled with plenty of cherries, chocolate, and a hint of almonds. This recipe combines the black forest cake flavors we love into a cherry and chocolate brownie that only takes a few minutes to stir together. With a dollop of whipped cream and some shaved chocolate over the top, this dessert happily satisfies our craving for the much more labor-intensive black forest cake.

¼ cup (60 g) butter

1¾ cups (294 g) semi-sweet chocolate chips, divided

½ cup (100 g) light brown sugar

1 tsp vanilla extract

1 tsp almond extract

2 eggs

¾ cup (93 g) all-purpose flour

¼ tsp kosher salt

1 (15-oz [430-g]) can of cherries in water, drained well

Whipped cream, for serving (optional)

Preheat the oven to 325°F (163°C). Line an 8-inch (20-cm) square pan with parchment paper.

Melt the butter in a large saucepan, over medium heat. When the butter has melted completely, add 1 cup (168 g) of the chocolate chips and stir until they have melted. Remove from the heat, add the brown sugar, and stir to combine.

Add the vanilla, almond extract, and the eggs and stir until smooth and shiny. Add the flour and salt and stir to combine. Stir in ¼ cup (42 g) of the remaining chocolate chips. Gently stir in the cherries. Spread the batter in the prepared pan and sprinkle with the remaining ½ cup (84 g) of chocolate chips.

Bake for 30 to 32 minutes, or until an inserted toothpick shows moist crumbs—be careful not to overcook or the brownies will be dry. Let them cool completely before slicing. Serve topped with whipped cream, if desired.

Baker's Note: For this recipe, I use canned cherries in water. This is NOT the same thing as cherry pie filling. However, you can also use fresh sweet cherries that have been pitted and sliced in half. Frozen cherries will work as well; however, you'll want to thaw them enough to slice them in half or quarter them, depending on their size.

IRISH COFFEE BARS

Yield: 9–12 bars	Buttery rich bars sweet from brown sugar, slightly crunchy with pecans, and balanced with plenty of coffee flavor and a tiny splash of Irish cream liqueur, these bars are amazing with a cup of coffee or hot tea.

FOR THE BARS
½ cup (120 g) butter

1 tbsp (7 g) instant coffee

⅔ cup (135 g) light brown sugar

⅓ cup (65 g) white sugar

1 egg

1 tsp vanilla extract

1 cup (125 g) all-purpose flour

½ tsp cinnamon

½ tsp baking soda

¼ tsp salt

¾ cup (84 g) chopped pecans

FOR THE GLAZE
½ cup (50 g) powdered sugar

1–2 tbsp (15–30 ml) Irish cream liqueur

Preheat the oven to 350°F (177°C). Line an 8-inch (20-cm) square pan with parchment paper or grease well with butter.

To make the bars, melt the butter over medium high heat in a medium-size saucepan. When the butter has melted, remove from the heat and add the coffee. Stir to dissolve. Add the brown sugar and white sugar and stir to combine. Add the egg and vanilla. Stir to combine. Stir in the flour, cinnamon, baking soda, and salt, until just combined. Add the pecans. Stir to mix throughout.

Scoop the batter into the prepared pan and spread to the sides with a spatula. Bake for 22 to 26 minutes, or until the top is lightly browned and cracked on the edges and an inserted toothpick has moist crumbs. The bars will still be soft when removed from the oven. Cool completely before slicing into bars.

To make the glaze, whisk together the powdered sugar and 1 tablespoon (15 ml) of the Irish cream liqueur. Add a tiny bit more liqueur, only as needed to achieve a thick, pourable glaze. Drizzle the glaze over the cooled bars. Let the bars dry before storing in an airtight container.

Baker's Notes: This recipe can be doubled to fill a 9 x 13–inch (23 x 33–cm) pan. The doubled recipe will need to be baked for 40 to 45 minutes, or until an inserted toothpick has moist crumbs. Slice into 16 to 24 bars.

I use 1 (0.11-oz [3-g]) tube of instant coffee (the kind from a well-known coffee shop) for the 1-tablespoon (7-g) portion listed in this recipe.

Heavy cream or milk may be substituted for the Irish cream liqueur in this recipe. I enjoy the subtle flavor that the liqueur adds, but the bars are also delicious without it.

KITCHEN SINK BLONDIES

Yield:
9–12 bars

"Kitchen sink" recipes typically contain an assortment of random odds and ends found in the pantry or refrigerator. These blondies started as a late-night craving a while back, and since then, they've become a popular salty-sweet treat for our movie nights.

When you want something fun and a little unexpected to eat, these bars absolutely fit that craving. Use whichever ingredients you have on hand. A total of about 3 cups (400 to 500 g) of add-ins, with a good balance of salty and sweet, is perfect.

½ cup (120 g) butter, melted

1 cup (200 g) light brown sugar

1 egg

2 tsp (10 ml) vanilla extract

1 cup (125 g) all-purpose flour

¼ tsp salt

½ cup (84 g) semi-sweet chocolate chunks

½ cup (84 g) dark chocolate chips

½ cup (55 g) chopped pecans

1 cup (100 g) potato chips with ridges, crushed into ½–1-inch (1.3–2.5-cm) pieces

½ cup (84 g) caramel bits

Preheat the oven to 350°F (177°C). Line an 8-inch (20-cm) square pan with parchment paper or grease well with butter.

Combine the butter and sugar in a large bowl and stir until smooth. Add the egg and vanilla and stir to combine. Stir in the flour and salt, until just combined. Add the chocolate chunks, chocolate chips, pecans, and potato chips. Stir to mix throughout. Scoop the batter into the prepared pan and spread to the sides with a spatula. Scatter the caramel bits on top.

Bake for 25 to 28 minutes, or until slightly browned around the edges and an inserted toothpick has moist crumbs. The top of the blondies should be slightly cracked on top. Cool completely before slicing into bars.

Baker's Notes: This recipe can be doubled to fill a 9 x 13–inch (23 x 33–cm) pan. The doubled recipe will need to be baked for 40 to 45 minutes, or until an inserted toothpick has moist crumbs. Slice into 16 to 24 bars.

For the best-looking final result, set aside 1 to 2 tablespoons (10 to 21 g) each of the chocolate chunks, chocolate chips, pecans, potato chips, and caramel bits. Sprinkle the reserved add-ins on top of the blondies before baking.

Cobblers, Crisps, Crumbles, and Flops

Cobblers, crisps, crumbles, and flops are baked desserts filled with fruit and topped with a pastry, streusel, or oat-filled crust. Wondering what the difference is between them? Cobblers have a sweet biscuit topping. While crisps and crumbles are very similar, traditionally, the main difference has been that crisps contain oats and crumbles do not. Still wondering about that "flop?" While the name may be unusual, this is one of the easiest desserts in the book. To make Grandma's Old-Fashioned Fruit Flop (page 128), you pour the topping into the pan first and then spoon fruit on top of it. As it bakes, the topping will "flop" over on top of the fruit. Flops are as fun as they sound and are the ultimate low-maintenance fruit desserts.

With these recipes, you get all of the awesomeness of a fruit dessert with the ease of recipes using frozen or canned fruit. I'm a huge fan of using fresh fruits whenever possible, but there are times when the convenience of having fruits stashed in the freezer or pantry can't be beat. The ease with which you can deliver big-time flavor ensures that these desserts will be a major hit, whether you're making Lemon-Blueberry Cobbler (page 119), Cherries and Chocolate Almond Crisp (page 124), or Cranberry-Almond Crumble (page 131).

Here are some notes for the recipes in this chapter:

- Fresh fruits may be substituted in these recipes when they're delicious and in season, and I often do that when I have a little more prep time available. However, I promise that making these desserts with the frozen or canned fruits listed in the recipes will not disappoint.

- While they come together in a hurry, don't rush these in the oven. These desserts are not done until the fruit is bubbly. Don't expect the filling to be sturdy like pies, though. That extra juiciness is one of the beautiful things about this category of desserts.

- Be sure to use the pan that is specified in the recipe. Going with a smaller pan will crowd the topping, which basically steams your fruit instead of roasting or baking it, making for a wet, unsatisfying topping. Conversely, going with a pan that is too large will make the recipe bake far faster, allowing too much liquid to evaporate and landing you with a dry, sad fruit dessert with no luscious sauce to spoon over ice cream.

- The easiest way to top a cobbler is to reach for one of those cookie scoops that I told you about in the cookie chapter (page 45)! Dropping the topping over the fruit with a cookie scoop helps you cover the pan evenly (and quickly) without disturbing the fruit underneath and yields a beautiful finished cobbler.

Scoop these desserts into bowls while they're still warm and top with ice cream or whipped cream. However you serve them, you're going to love them.

LEMON-BLUEBERRY COBBLER

Yield:	Juicy blueberries in a sweet lemon sauce fill this flaky buttery cobbler. I like to serve this cobbler
6 servings	with a scoop of whipped cream and a generous drizzle of warm lemon curd. This dessert reheats
	nicely and it also doubles as a favorite ice cream add-in (see page 144).

FOR THE FILLING
Butter, for pan

16 oz (455 g) frozen blueberries

¼ cup (50 g) white sugar

2 tbsp (16 g) cornstarch

½ cup (120 ml) lemon curd, plus more for topping

FOR THE CRUST TOPPING
3 tbsp (36 g) white sugar

1 tbsp (4 g) finely minced lemon zest

¾ cup (93 g) all-purpose flour

3 tbsp (38 g) light brown sugar

½ tsp baking powder

¼ tsp kosher salt

¼ cup (60 g) cold butter

¼ cup (60 ml) boiling water

Whipped cream, for serving

Preheat the oven to 375°F (191°C). Grease an 8-inch (20-cm) round or square baking pan or an 8-inch (20-cm) cast-iron skillet with butter.

To make the filling, combine the blueberries, sugar, and cornstarch in a large bowl. Stir to coat. Warm the lemon curd in the microwave until it's smooth and stirrable. Add the lemon curd to the blueberry mixture and stir to coat. Pour into the prepared pan.

To make the crust topping, combine the white sugar and lemon zest in a large bowl and rub with your fingers to mix well. Add the flour, brown sugar, baking powder, and salt and stir to combine. Grate the cold butter and add the butter shreds to the flour mixture and toss. Stir in the boiling water, until just combined, leaving plenty of little lumps of butter. Drop spoonfuls of the topping over the berries.

Bake for about 34 to 36 minutes, or until the crust is golden and a toothpick inserted into the crust comes out clean. Serve warm or at room temperature, topped with whipped cream and a drizzle of warm lemon curd.

Baker's Notes: This may also be made with fresh berries. When using fresh berries, reduce the baking time as needed by 3 to 4 minutes and remove from the oven when the crust has baked through.

Lemon curd can be found in most grocery stores near the jellies and jams, typically on the top shelf.

CARAMEL APPLE–WALNUT CRUMBLE

Yield:
6 servings

Caramel apple slices and a crunchy walnut streusel topping combine to make this crumble the irresistible treat that it is. This is an extra-sweet dessert, so I typically serve fairly small amounts of the crumble along with a scoop of ice cream. My boys love this dessert so much that, given the chance, they will devour the whole pan as soon as it's cool enough to eat.

FOR THE FILLING
Butter, for dish

5 medium apples, sliced thin
(approximately 6 cups [654 g])

¼ cup (50 g) light brown sugar

1 tsp cornstarch

¼ tsp kosher salt

¼ cup (60 ml) caramel sauce, plus
more for serving

FOR THE CRUMBLE TOPPING
1¼ cups (156 g) all-purpose flour

½ cup (55 g) walnuts, chopped

½ cup (100 g) light brown sugar

¾ cup (180 g) butter, melted

Ice cream, for serving

Preheat the oven to 375°F (191°C). Grease an 8-inch (20-cm) square baking dish with butter.

To make the filling, place the apples in the prepared baking dish and sprinkle with the brown sugar, cornstarch, and salt. Toss with your hands to coat. Drizzle with the caramel sauce.

To make the crumble topping, stir together the flour, walnuts, and brown sugar in a medium bowl. Add the melted butter and stir to combine. Sprinkle the topping over the apples. Bake for 22 minutes, or until the crust has lightly browned. Serve warm, drizzled with caramel sauce, and topped with ice cream.

Baker's Notes: I typically use Granny Smith apples to make this crumble. Feel free to use your favorite baking apple.

Store-bought caramel sauce or the Salted-Vanilla Caramel Sauce on page 159 will work for this recipe.

BROWN SUGAR–PEACH COBBLER

Yield: 4 servings	Brown sugar adds a depth of flavor to the syrupy peaches in this cobbler. With a sweet shortbread biscuit topping, this cobbler comes together in just a few minutes. I like to make this in individual ramekins for a special treat, but it also works well in an 8-inch (20-cm) square pan.

FOR THE FILLING
Butter, for ramekins

16 oz (455 g) frozen peaches, roughly chopped if making individual cobblers

1 tbsp (15 ml) fresh lemon juice

¼ cup (50 g) light brown sugar

¼ tsp cinnamon

⅛ tsp nutmeg

1 tbsp (8 g) cornstarch

FOR THE CRUST TOPPING
1 cup (125 g) all-purpose flour

½ cup (100 g) light brown sugar

1 tsp baking powder

½ tsp kosher salt

½ cup (120 ml) heavy cream, plus extra if needed

FOR THE CINNAMON-SUGAR TOPPING
1½ tbsp (18 g) sugar

½ tsp cinnamon

Preheat the oven to 375°F (191°C). Grease 4 large ramekins (6 to 8 ounces [180 to 240 ml]) with butter and place them on a baking sheet.

To make the filling, combine the peaches, lemon juice, brown sugar, cinnamon, nutmeg, and cornstarch in a large bowl. Toss to coat.

To make the crust topping, combine the flour, brown sugar, baking powder, and salt in a medium bowl. Pour the cream into the flour mixture and stir with a fork to combine. Drizzle more cream in only as needed to achieve a biscuit dough–like consistency.

Divide the peach filling into the prepared ramekins. Use your hands to drop the crust topping over the peaches. Stir together the sugar and cinnamon for the topping. Sprinkle evenly over the cobbler. Bake for 28 minutes, or until the crust is golden and a toothpick inserted into the crust comes out clean. Serve warm or at room temperature.

Baker's Notes: Fresh peaches may be substituted for frozen when in season.

This cobbler can be made in an 8-inch (20-cm) square pan and baked for 38 to 42 minutes. Check both the mini cobblers and the larger pan cobbler about 5 minutes before the recommended time. The times listed are for frozen fruit. If your fruit has partially thawed, or if you're using fresh fruit, the cobblers will bake faster.

CHERRIES AND CHOCOLATE ALMOND CRISP

Yield: 6 servings	Cherries, almonds, and a sprinkling of dark chocolate are tucked into this irresistible fruit crisp. Serve this one warm with a melting scoop of vanilla or chocolate ice cream for a crisp like no other. I like to drizzle a bit of the juices from the cobbler over the top of the ice cream as well.

FOR THE FILLING
Butter, for dish

16 oz (455 g) frozen cherries

¼ cup (50 g) light brown sugar

½ tsp almond extract

2 tbsp (16 g) cornstarch

¼ tsp kosher salt

¼ cup (42 g) dark chocolate chips

FOR THE TOPPING
½ cup (62 g) all-purpose flour

½ cup (40 g) old-fashioned rolled oats

¼ cup (23 g) sliced almonds

⅓ cup (67 g) light brown sugar

6 tbsp (90 g) butter, melted

Ice cream or whipped cream, for serving (optional)

Preheat the oven to 375°F (191°C). Grease an 8-inch (20-cm) square baking dish with butter.

To make the filling, place the cherries in a large bowl. Add the sugar, almond extract, cornstarch, and salt. Stir to combine and then pour the filling into the prepared baking dish. Scatter chocolate chips over the cherries and stir just a little bit to create an uneven layer with plenty of dips for the crisp topping to fill.

To make the topping, stir together the flour, oats, almonds, and brown sugar in a medium bowl. Add the melted butter and stir to combine. Sprinkle the topping over the fruit. Bake for 28 minutes, or until the crust turns golden brown. Serve warm from the oven. Top with vanilla ice cream or whipped cream if desired.

Baker's Note: The chocolate is not required for this recipe, but that little bit of dark chocolate does add an extra something special. Feel free to skip it, if it isn't your thing. The crisp is delicious without it as well.

MINI PECAN-PEAR CRISPS

Yield:
4 servings

Juicy pears in a cinnamon-sugar sauce are tucked under a pecan crisp topping that is sweet and crunchy. With a scoop of ice cream on top or completely on its own, my kids go crazy over this dessert.

While fresh pears are lovely, their season is brief, and the convenience of an easy fruit dessert you can make with pears from the pantry cannot be beat. This is another great dessert for individual serving dishes. The juices from the pears collect nicely in the smaller dishes.

FOR THE FILLING
Butter, for dishes

2 (15-oz [430-g]) cans sliced pears, drained well

1 tbsp (15 ml) fresh lemon juice

3 tbsp (38 g) light brown sugar

1 tbsp (8 g) cornstarch

½ tsp cinnamon

¼ tsp kosher salt

½ tsp vanilla extract

FOR THE TOPPING
¼ cup (31 g) all-purpose flour

½ cup (40 g) old-fashioned rolled oats

¼ cup (28 g) chopped pecans

½ cup (100 g) light brown sugar

⅓ cup (80 g) butter, melted

Preheat the oven to 375°F (191°C). Place four oven-safe baking dishes (6–8 ounces [180–240 ml]) on a baking tray and grease with butter.

To make the filling, place the pears on a cutting board and roughly chop them into bite-size pieces. Transfer to a large bowl and add the lemon juice, brown sugar, cornstarch, cinnamon, salt, and vanilla. Stir to combine. Divide the pear mixture among the prepared baking dishes.

To make the topping, stir together the flour, oats, pecans, and brown sugar in a medium bowl. Add the melted butter and stir to combine. Sprinkle the topping over the pears. Bake for 15 minutes, or until the crust turns golden brown. Serve warm or at room temperature.

Baker's Note: This may also be made in an 8-inch (20-cm) square baking dish. Increase the baking time by 5 to 6 minutes, as needed, or until the crust turns golden.

GRANDMA'S OLD-FASHIONED FRUIT FLOP

Yield:
6 servings

A flop is a fairly simple, fluffy, cake-like treat filled with chunks of fruit—similar to a dump cake. This cherry flop was my Grandma Zintz's claim to fame in the kitchen, and it was her go-to dessert recipe. Grandma was not known for her cooking and baking skills, but she pulled this dessert together for company for more years than I can remember. As the story goes, she misread the directions the first time she made it, and the crust flipped over onto the top of the fruit. However it came to be made, the "flop" was a hit, and she continued making it the same way.

Grandma always made this dessert with cherries; however, I've discovered that the recipe works well with almost any canned fruit. Make sure you really love the fruit you use, because it will be the dominant flavor in this dessert.

¾ cup (93 g) all-purpose flour

¼ cup (50 g) white sugar

1 tsp baking powder

½ tsp cinnamon

¼ tsp kosher salt

½ cup (120 ml) milk

¼ cup (60 g) butter, melted

2 (15-oz [430-g]) cans fruit in light or heavy syrup

Vanilla ice cream, for serving

Preheat the oven to 350°F (177°C). Grease an 8-inch (20-cm) round or square baking dish with butter.

In a large bowl, combine the flour, sugar, baking powder, cinnamon, and salt and whisk to combine. Add the milk and whisk smooth. Add the butter and whisk. Pour the batter into the prepared dish and spread to the edges of the pan. Drain the fruit, reserving ½ cup (120 ml) total of liquid. Spoon the fruit across the batter and then pour the reserved liquid over the top.

Bake for 38 to 44 minutes, or until golden on top and a toothpick inserted comes out mostly clean without any wet batter on it. Scoop the warm fruit flop into bowls and top with vanilla ice cream.

Baker's Notes: This dessert is best served within one hour of baking.

Frozen fruits will not work for this recipe. The juices from the canned fruits are required in order to have enough moisture in this dessert.

CRANBERRY-ALMOND CRUMBLE

Yield:
6–8 servings

Tart cranberries and a sweet almond crumble topping are an irresistible combination. The buttery, sweet, and tart combination in this dessert makes it a holiday favorite. I recommend stashing a few bags of cranberries in the freezer so that you'll be able to enjoy this dessert throughout the year.

FOR THE FILLING
¼ cup (60 g) butter, melted, plus more for pan

12 oz (340 g) fresh or frozen cranberries

¾ cup (150 g) light brown sugar

3 tbsp (24 g) cornstarch

½ tsp ground ginger

½ tsp ground cinnamon

¼ tsp kosher salt

½ tsp almond extract

FOR THE TOPPING
1¼ cups (156 g) all-purpose flour

½ cup (50 g) sliced almonds

⅔ cup (135 g) light brown sugar

10 tbsp (148 g) butter, melted

Preheat the oven to 375°F (191°C). Grease an 8-inch (20-cm) square pan with butter.

To make the filling, combine the cranberries, brown sugar, cornstarch, ginger, cinnamon, salt, and almond extract in a large bowl. Stir to combine. Drizzle with the butter and stir again to coat. Pour the cranberry mixture into the prepared baking dish.

To make the topping, combine the flour, almonds, and brown sugar in a large bowl. Add the melted butter and stir with a fork to combine and create large crumbs. Sprinkle the topping over the fruit. Bake for 26 to 28 minutes, or until the topping turns golden brown. Serve warm or at room temperature.

Baker's Notes: Yes, there is a good amount of sugar in this recipe. It works to balance the extreme tartness of fresh cranberries.

This may be made either with fresh or frozen cranberries. The frozen cranberries may be added to the recipe without thawing.

BERRIES AND CREAM COBBLER

Yield:
6 servings

Sweet berries are combined with a creamy filling and then topped with a flaky cobbler crust to make this dessert. My youngest son loves this cobbler, and he'll hover next to it as it cools, just to be the first one to "taste test" it. Take care not to stir the cream cheese mixture into the fruit, as you want the separate flavors of fruit and sweet cream cheese in each bite.

FOR THE FILLING
Butter, for greasing pan

16 oz (455 g) frozen assorted berries

½ cup (100 g) white sugar, divided

2 tbsp (16 g) cornstarch

½ tsp cinnamon

¼ tsp cardamom

4 oz (115 g) cream cheese, room temperature

2 tbsp (30 ml) heavy cream

FOR THE TOPPING
¾ cup (93 g) all-purpose flour

3 tbsp (38 g) light brown sugar

3 tbsp (36 g) white sugar

½ tsp baking powder

¼ tsp kosher salt

⅓ cup (80 ml) heavy cream, plus additional if needed

Whipped cream, for serving (optional)

Preheat the oven to 400°F (204°C). Grease an 8-inch (20-cm) round or square baking pan or a 10-inch (25-cm) cast-iron skillet with butter.

To make the filling, place the berries in the prepared baking dish. Sprinkle with ¼ cup (50 g) of the sugar, cornstarch, cinnamon, and cardamom. Stir to coat. In a medium bowl, combine the cream cheese and the remaining ¼ cup (50 g) of sugar and beat until smooth. Add the heavy cream and beat again until smooth and creamy. Drop spoonfuls of the cream cheese mixture over the berries.

To make the topping, combine the flour, brown sugar, sugar, baking powder, and salt in a medium bowl and stir to combine. Pour in the cream and stir with a fork until just combined. Drizzle in more cream only if needed. The batter should resemble biscuit dough.

Drop spoonfuls of the topping over the berries and cream cheese. Bake for 28 to 38 minutes, or until the crust is golden and a toothpick inserted into the crust comes out clean. Serve warm or at room temperature, topped with whipped cream, if desired.

Baker's Note: The humidity in the weather will affect how much additional cream needs to be added to this recipe. Add the cream slowly, just until the topping comes together.

BOURBON APRICOT OR PEACH CRISP

<table>
<tr><td>Yield:
6–8 servings</td><td>When apricots are in season, this recipe is one of my favorite ways to use them. However, any stone fruit will work beautifully in this crisp. This is the only recipe in this chapter made with fresh fruit; however, when stone fruits aren't at the peak of the season (or pretty much any other time I want to make this on a whim), I frequently make this crisp with frozen peaches.</td></tr>
</table>

FOR THE FILLING
Butter, for greasing dish

4 cups (450 g) quartered fresh apricots, or 16 oz (455 g) frozen peaches, slightly thawed

¼ cup (60 ml) bourbon

¼ cup (50 g) light brown sugar

1 tsp cinnamon

1 tbsp (8 g) cornstarch

½ tsp kosher salt

1 tsp vanilla extract

FOR THE TOPPING
¾ cup (93 g) all-purpose flour

¾ cup (60 g) old-fashioned rolled oats

½ cup (100 g) raw sugar

¼ tsp ground cinnamon

½ cup (120 g) butter, melted

Vanilla ice cream, for serving (optional)

Preheat the oven to 375°F (191°C). Grease an 8-inch (20-cm) baking dish or 10-inch (25-cm) oven-safe skillet with butter.

To make the filling, place the fruit in a bowl. Add the bourbon, brown sugar, cinnamon, cornstarch, salt, and vanilla. Stir to combine and set aside.

To make the topping, stir together the flour, oats, sugar, and cinnamon in a large bowl. Add the melted butter and stir to combine. Pour the fruit and all of its liquid into the prepared dish and sprinkle the topping over the fruit. Bake for 30 to 35 minutes, or until the crust turns golden brown. Serve warm from the oven, and top with vanilla ice cream if desired.

Baker's Note: The raw sugar in the crust adds a hint of crunch to the recipe and a slightly different flavor. Light brown sugar may be swapped for the raw sugar in the crust. It works well both ways.

OATMEAL-RAISIN APPLE CRISP

Yield:
6 servings

Tender baked apples mixed with a crisp oatmeal and raisin streusel is a combination that I can't resist. This crisp tastes like a bowl of your favorite oatmeal kicked up to a whole new level. It's like a warm granola filled with apples, as opposed to a liquid-filled crisp. We enjoy serving it with ice cream, whipped cream, or simply a drizzle of heavy cream.

Butter, for greasing dish

2 cups (160 g) old-fashioned rolled oats

1 cup (125 g) all-purpose flour

¾ cup (150 g) light brown sugar

½ tsp cinnamon

½ tsp nutmeg

¼ tsp kosher salt

¾ cup (180 g) butter, melted

5 medium apples, thinly sliced (approximately 5–6 cups [545–654 g])

½ cup (60 g) raisins

Ice cream, for serving (optional)

Preheat the oven to 375°F (191°C). Grease a 2.5-quart (2.5-L) baking dish or a 10-inch (25-cm) cast-iron skillet with butter.

Combine the oats, flour, brown sugar, cinnamon, nutmeg, and salt in a large bowl. Drizzle with the melted butter and stir with a fork to create large crumbs. Add the apples and the raisins and use your hands to mix well.

Transfer to the prepared baking dish. Bake for 26 minutes, or until the topping is golden brown and the apples are tender. Serve with ice cream, if desired.

Baker's Note: I typically use Granny Smith or Pink Lady apples when baking. Feel free to use your favorite.

PINEAPPLE-COCONUT CRISP

<table>
<tr><td>Yield:
8 servings</td><td>Sweet pineapple and coconut combine in this tropical twist on a classic crisp. Topped with ice cream, this is a terrific variation on a traditional fruit crisp. I love serving this warm, so grab a spoon and dig in while it's hot.</td></tr>
</table>

FOR THE FILLING

4 cups (560 g) frozen pineapple chunks

2 tbsp (16 g) cornstarch

¼ cup (50 g) light brown sugar

½ tsp ground ginger

¼ tsp ground cinnamon

FOR THE TOPPING

¾ cup (60 g) old-fashioned rolled oatmeal

½ cup (47 g) shredded sweetened coconut

½ cup (62 g) all-purpose flour

¼ cup (50 g) light brown sugar

½ tsp ground ginger

¼ tsp ground cinnamon

¼ tsp kosher salt

½ cup (120 g) butter, melted

Whipped cream or ice cream, for serving (optional)

Preheat the oven to 375°F (191°C). Lightly grease an 8-inch (20-cm) baking dish.

To make the filling, place the pineapple chunks in the baking dish. Sprinkle with the cornstarch, brown sugar, ginger, and cinnamon. Stir to combine.

To make the topping, combine the oatmeal, coconut, flour, brown sugar, ginger, cinnamon, and salt in a large bowl. Add the butter and stir with a fork to combine and create large crumbs. Sprinkle the crumb topping over the pineapple. Bake for 25 to 28 minutes, or until golden brown. Let it cool a few minutes before serving. Top with whipped cream or ice cream, if desired.

Baker's Note: This recipe works beautifully with fresh pineapple as well as with frozen. However, I do not recommend making this recipe with canned pineapple.

Irresistible Ice Creams, Puddings, and Sauces

It's no secret that I am now and always will be an ice cream–loving girl. Ice cream will always be the dessert that I turn to first, because it is just so perfect. I am super excited to give you my Best and Easiest Vanilla Ice Cream recipe (page 143) that has been made by thousands of readers who turn to it again and again.

And while the vanilla ice cream is positively perfect in every way, there's always room for fun, and I've included four fabulous ways to mix it up and keep it exciting. My ice cream maker is probably the most frequently used appliance in the kitchen, and I can't recommend one highly enough. There is nothing better than homemade ice cream for a dessert that everyone loves.

As for puddings, I haven't always found them to be thrilling, until I started this book, and I am happy to tell you that the puddings in this book changed my mind. These have all earned a place in my regular dessert rotation, and when you taste them, you will understand why. Light and Creamy Lemon Pudding (page 151), Seven-Minute Dark Chocolate Pudding (page 148), and Salted Butterscotch Pudding (page 152) are, in two words, pretty amazing. And I cannot wait for you to try them.

For those date nights or special occasions, I have a Raspberry Creme Brûlée (page 155) that will set the tone just right. It is easy and delicious enough to make you want more special occasions.

I haven't forgotten the toppings, either! You'll enjoy the Perfect-Every-Time Hot Fudge Sauce (page 156), Salted-Vanilla Caramel Sauce (page 159), and Five-Minute Berry Sauce (page 160) that are so good that you may forego a dessert under them and just spoon them from the pan or jar. A word of advice, though . . . don't spoon the piping-hot fudge or salted caramel directly from the pan. Trust me.

These are all simple, but I'd like to remind you to use the pan size that is called for in the recipes. There is no cleanup job quite like the one that awaits you if your caramel or hot fudge sauces boil over onto your cooktop. And much like the sauces and their pans, you want to avoid overfilling your ice cream maker, no matter which type you have. These recipes are designed for a 1½-quart (1.5-L) ice cream maker. So if yours is smaller, you may want to run the recipes through it in two batches.

BEST AND EASIEST VANILLA ICE CREAM

Yield:
5 servings

Rich and creamy homemade ice cream is a treat few people can resist. Lucky for all of us, this ice cream recipe is dead simple and once you've made it, you'll be stirring it together whenever you're craving a cold sweet treat. I've made this ice cream countless times over the past few years, and more often than not, I skip the simmering step that I mention in the Baker's Note. It is, admittedly, even creamier ice cream if you do simmer and chill the base prior to freezing.

1⅔ cups (400 ml) heavy cream

1⅓ cups (320 ml) whole milk

¾ cup (150 g) white sugar

⅛ tsp kosher salt

1 tbsp (15 ml) vanilla extract

Combine the cream, milk, sugar, salt, and vanilla in a large bowl. Whisk well to combine and immediately pour into the ice cream maker. Churn according to the manufacturer's instructions.

Transfer the finished ice cream to an airtight container and place in the freezer until ready to serve.

Baker's Note: If you have a few extra minutes and think of it a few hours before you want to make the ice cream, you can bring all the ingredients, except the vanilla, to a simmer in a small saucepan. Stir or whisk until the sugar has melted completely. Add the vanilla and then chill the ice cream base until it is cold again before churning the ice cream in the machine.

FOUR TASTY WAYS TO MIX UP VANILLA ICE CREAM

Yield:
4–6 servings

While the Best and Easiest Vanilla Ice Cream (page 143) is already perfect on its own, we love mixing things up to create more fun new ice cream flavors.

These are four delicious combinations that my family loves. When your ice cream has finished churning, follow the directions below to add in your chosen flavor combination. Once you've learned how to make homemade ice cream, you'll be stirring together your own specialty flavors in no time.

CHOCOLATE CHIP CHERRY CRISP ICE CREAM
½ batch Cherries and Chocolate Almond Crisp (page 124), refrigerated until firm and then chopped into bite-size pieces

½ cup (84 g) mini chocolate chips

OATMEAL COOKIE ICE CREAM
5–6 Favorite Oatmeal Raisin Cookies (page 60), chopped into ½-inch (1.3-cm) pieces (approximately 3 cups [75 g])

LEMON-BLUEBERRY COBBLER ICE CREAM
½ batch Lemon-Blueberry Cobbler (page 119), refrigerated until firm and then chopped into bite-size pieces

½ cup (120 ml) lemon curd

KITCHEN SINK ICE CREAM
4 Kitchen Sink Blondies (page 114), chopped into ½-inch (1.3-cm) pieces

¼ cup (60 ml) Salted-Vanilla Caramel Sauce (page 159)

¼ cup (60 ml) Perfect-Every-Time Hot Fudge Sauce (page 156)

IMPORTANT TIPS FOR MIXING IN ICE CREAM ADD-INS
Stir the ice cream as little as possible.

Sprinkle one-third of the add-ins across the bottom of an ice cream storage container. Scoop half of the ice cream over the add-ins. Layer with another third of the add-ins and then scoop the remaining ice cream into the container. Top with the remaining add-ins.

When adding a liquid such as hot fudge, caramel, berry sauce, or lemon curd, make sure it is room temperature or slightly chilled. Drizzle it on top and then lightly swirl with a knife to mix throughout and create ribbons of that ingredient through the ice cream.

When adding cobblers and crisps, refrigerate them first. Chop the cold dessert into small pieces before adding it to the ice cream. You can then swirl in a liquid after, per the tip above, if desired.

FRESH STRAWBERRY ICE CREAM

Yield:
5–6 servings

Strawberries with sweet cream is an irresistible combination. This ice cream is about as easy as can be to make, and we make it often. Combine all of the ingredients in the blender, puree, and pour into the ice cream maker. That's all there is to it. You'll be enjoying homemade ice cream in no time at all.

1 lb (455 g) fresh sweet strawberries, washed and tops removed

½ cup (120 ml) whole milk

1 cup (240 ml) heavy cream

1 (14-oz [420-ml]) can sweetened condensed milk

2 tsp (10 ml) vanilla extract

¼ tsp kosher salt

Place the berries and the milk in a blender. Blend to combine. Add the cream, condensed milk, vanilla, and salt. Blend until smooth. Pour the mixture into your ice cream maker and churn according to the manufacturer's directions.

Baker's Notes: I emphasize "sweet" strawberries in the ingredients list because the ice cream will only be as flavorful as the berries that you use in the recipe.

You may use frozen (fully thawed) berries in this recipe; however, the result won't be quite as predictable as with fresh berries that you are able to taste before using.

SEVEN-MINUTE DARK CHOCOLATE PUDDING

Yield:
2–4 servings

It only takes a few minutes to make homemade pudding from scratch. And once you've tried it you may never want to buy a box of pudding mix again. This rich and creamy chocolate pudding is absolutely nothing like store-bought pudding, and I finally understand the fuss some people make over the wonders of homemade pudding.

½ cup (100 g) white sugar

1½ tbsp (12 g) cornstarch

1½ cups (360 ml) whole milk

⅔ cup (112 g) dark chocolate chips

½ tsp vanilla extract

¼ tsp kosher salt

Combine the sugar and cornstarch in a medium saucepan. Whisk to combine. Add the milk and whisk again. Bring to a boil over high heat and reduce to simmer. Continue stirring constantly until thickened and smooth, about 3 minutes. Remove from the heat. Add the chocolate chips and stir until melted and smooth. Add the vanilla and salt. Stir to combine. Serve warm or refrigerate until ready to serve.

Variation: Add a dash of cayenne pepper or red chile powder to the milk as it heats. This will provide a nice hint of heat to the pudding.

LIGHT AND CREAMY LEMON PUDDING

Yield:
2 servings

Cream + sugar + lemon = all you need to make one of my favorite desserts. This is a very simple pudding recipe that works almost magically. The acid in the lemon reacts with the cream and sugar to thicken the pudding as it chills in the refrigerator. Once cold, you'll be dipping your spoon into a creamy, smooth lemon dessert like nothing you've had before.

1 cup (240 ml) heavy cream

⅓ cup (65 g) white sugar

3 tbsp (45 ml) fresh lemon juice

½ tsp finely minced lemon zest

Whisk together the cream and sugar in a medium saucepan. Bring to a boil over high heat, while stirring frequently. Allow the creamy mixture to boil over medium heat for about 2 minutes while stirring constantly. Add the lemon juice and zest. Reduce the heat and continue stirring over a low boil until slightly thickened, about 2 minutes. The mixture should still be quite thin and pourable.

Pour into serving bowls and refrigerate for 2 to 3 hours or until ready to serve. The pudding will set while it rests and cools in the refrigerator.

Baker's Note: This recipe is written for two generous servings. However, it multiplies perfectly to make as many servings as you might like.

SALTED BUTTERSCOTCH PUDDING

Yield:
2 servings

Have I mentioned often enough how much I love a sprinkling of salt on a sweet dessert? This pudding is an excellent example of just how wonderfully the creamy butterscotch pudding is complemented by a little bit of salt.

¼ cup (50 g) dark brown sugar

1 tbsp (8 g) cornstarch

½ cup (120 ml) heavy cream

½ cup (120 ml) whole milk

½ tsp vanilla extract

Sea salt flakes, such as Maldon salt, or coarse sea salt (optional)

Combine the sugar and cornstarch in a medium saucepan. Whisk to combine. Add the cream and milk and whisk again. Bring to a boil over high heat and immediately reduce to simmer as soon as bubbles form. Continue stirring constantly until thickened and smooth, about 3 to 5 minutes.

Remove from the heat. Add the vanilla and stir to combine. Pour into individual serving dishes or a large serving dish and refrigerate until ready to serve. Sprinkle with salt before serving, if desired.

Baker's Note: This recipe is written for two generous servings. However, it multiplies perfectly to make as many servings as you might like.

RASPBERRY CREME BRÛLÉE

Yield: 4 servings	Creamy rich custard, filled with sweet berries and then topped with a caramelized burnt sugar crust is about to become your new favorite "fancy" and oh-so-simple dessert. Creme brûlée never fails to impress, and once you've discovered just how easy it is to make, you're going to be in dessert heaven.

4 oz (115 g) fresh raspberries

2 cups (480 ml) heavy cream

1 vanilla bean, split and scraped, or 2 tsp (10 ml) vanilla extract

3 egg yolks

¼ cup (50 g) white sugar plus 4 tsp (16 g), divided

Water, to fill the baking pan halfway

Baker's Notes: Make sure the berries are completely and totally dry before pouring the cream mixture over them. Blackberries may be substituted for the raspberries in this recipe. Select small berries for this recipe. Unfortunately, this recipe will not work well with frozen berries.

While traditionally, creme brûlée requires tempering the eggs, this method eliminates that step.

Preheat the oven to 325°F (163°C). Place four oven-safe ramekins (3 to 4 ounces [90 to 120 ml]) or creme brûlée dishes in a baking pan with a deep rim. Place 4 berries in each ramekin. Add the cream and the vanilla bean to a saucepan over medium-high heat. Bring the mixture almost to a boil and then remove from the heat the moment you begin to see bubbles in the cream. Discard the vanilla bean.

In a medium bowl, whisk together the egg yolks and ¼ cup (50 g) of the white sugar until smooth. Slowly pour the warm cream into the egg mixture while whisking constantly to combine. Pour into the dishes with the berries.

Add water to the pan with the filled ramekins to about halfway up the sides of each dish. Place it on the middle oven rack and bake for 40 to 45 minutes. The creme brûlée should jiggle just a bit, but not appear to be watery. Carefully remove the very hot pan of water from the oven and let it cool for 10 minutes before transferring the dishes to the refrigerator to chill.

Refrigerate for at least 2 hours and up to 3 days. When ready to caramelize, set the dishes on a heat-resistant surface and let them warm to room temperature for about 30 minutes. Sprinkle each dish with about 1 teaspoon of sugar and then use a kitchen torch or the oven broiler to caramelize the sugar.

KITCHEN TORCH DIRECTIONS FOR CARAMELIZATION
Turn on the kitchen torch and slide it across the top of each dish until most of the sugar has melted, then let that cool while you repeat with the other dishes. Finish each dish with a second torching. Don't be afraid of slightly burning the tops, and make sure you get the sugar good and bubbling. Chill the finished creme brûlée once again until ready to serve.

OVEN DIRECTIONS FOR CARAMELIZATION
Move the top rack in your oven up as high as it will go. Place the ramekins in the oven on the top rack, and turn on the broiler. Broil for 2 to 5 minutes, rotating the ramekins frequently so that they broil evenly. Take them out when they are golden brown and bubbling. Chill the finished creme brûlée until ready to serve. Oven cooking times and temps vary greatly and what takes 5 or more minutes in one oven might only require 2 minutes in another oven. Stay next to the oven. Don't walk away.

PERFECT-EVERY-TIME HOT FUDGE SAUCE

Yield:
approximately
2½ cups
(600 ml)

Creamy, thick, rich, and chocolatey hot fudge is a dream (and often a must-have-in-the-house-at-all-times requirement) for any ice cream lover!

Years ago, my sister worked as a waitress at a restaurant known for serving the best comfort food in the area, and they made a brownie sundae that I could never resist. I love that with this sauce, I can recreate it at home.

This hot fudge sauce is perfect served warm, right off the stove. Because it only takes a few minutes to make, I like to make it right before I'm ready to make ice cream sundaes. If you set the ice cream on the counter when you start this sauce, it will be soft enough to scoop by the time the sauce is ready.

1½ cups (252 g) chocolate chips

1 (14-oz [420-ml]) can sweetened condensed milk

1 tsp vanilla or almond extract (optional)

Combine the chocolate chips and the condensed milk in a small saucepan over medium heat. Whisk constantly for 3 to 5 minutes, or until the chocolate has melted and the ingredients have combined smoothly. Watch the heat carefully so that the chocolate doesn't burn. Add the extract, if desired, and stir to combine. The sauce should be quite thick and will very slowly pour off a spoon. Serve warm and transfer any remaining sauce to an airtight container and refrigerate.

Baker's Notes: The hot fudge will firm up as it cools. Reheat it in the microwave (at half power), stirring frequently, until the sauce is smooth and stirrable once again.

Adding ½ cup (120 ml) of heavy cream along with the condensed milk will result in a thinner, more pourable sauce.

SALTED-VANILLA CARAMEL SAUCE

Yield:
about 1½ cups
(360 ml)

Smooth, creamy, buttery, sweet homemade caramel sauce is possible without spending your time stirring constantly over a hot stove. This sauce is quite thin when it finishes cooking on the stove, and it thickens as it cools. Straight from the refrigerator, it is still soft and scoopable. The sauce warms easily and is pourable at room temperature.

I love to serve the caramel warm, drizzled over fresh peaches, ice cream, brownies, cake . . . pretty much anything. There is nothing store-bought that can compete with homemade caramel sauce.

1 cup (200 g) white sugar

¼ cup (60 ml) water

½ cup (120 g) butter

2 tsp (10 ml) vanilla extract

¼ tsp kosher salt

½ cup (120 ml) heavy cream

In a heavy saucepan, combine the sugar and the water. Stir or swirl the pan to combine and then cook over medium heat for 5 minutes, or until the sugar dissolves. There is no need to stir; simply swirl the pan over the burner occasionally as the sugar dissolves.

Raise the heat to medium-high and cook the sugar water, swirling the pan occasionally, for 7 to 8 minutes, or until it is amber colored. It will go from amber to burnt in mere moments, so keep a close eye on the pan!

Add the butter (be prepared for it to bubble and sputter) and lightly stir or swirl to melt. Do not scrape the sides of the pan or splash sauce up the sides of the pan. Scraping uncooked sugar back into the sauce will cause crystallization.

Once the butter is melted, remove from the heat and add the vanilla, salt, and heavy cream. It will bubble again but will calm quickly. Whisk or stir to combine (again, not scraping the sides of the pan) and then let it cool completely before transferring to a jar and refrigerating for storage.

Baker's Note: For a stronger salted caramel flavor, increase the salt to ½ teaspoon.

FIVE-MINUTE BERRY SAUCE

Yield:
5 servings

Almost twenty years ago, while visiting a friend, we were dishing up bowls of ice cream and her husband told us to wait a minute. He combined some frozen fruit and a bit of sugar in a saucepan and simmered the mixture a few minutes. He poured the berry sauce over our bowls of ice cream and transformed them into something much more elegant.

I was speechless over the difference the warm fruit sauce made for that dish of ice cream. Lest you think this sauce is only good as an ice cream topping, it's also amazing over cheesecake, brownies, and cakes too. I stir it into yogurt, mix it into cheesecakes, and I've been known to eat it with a spoon straight from the refrigerator.

2 cups (460 g) frozen mixed berries

⅓ cup (65 g) white sugar

Place the frozen fruit and the sugar in a small saucepan. Set the heat to low, stirring occasionally, until the berries have softened. This should take between 5 and 10 minutes. Once the berries are mostly thawed, increase the heat to medium. Mash the berries with a potato masher and stir constantly while the liquid simmers for about 2 minutes.

Pour the warm mixture over vanilla ice cream or let it cool and then serve with the dessert of your choice. Store in the refrigerator until ready to use.

Baker's Note: I've made this simple topping countless times over the years, using whichever fruits I happened to have in the freezer at the time. A mix of different berries is my favorite combination as the different fruit flavors always combine so well together.

No-Bake Treats for Any Season

You may already know that I spent the past fifteen years living on the surface of the sun, also known as Phoenix, Arizona. While it's pure conjecture, I'm guessing a fellow Phoenix resident invented the category of no-bake desserts, because sometimes it is just way too hot to fire up that oven. Thank you, mystery no-baker, whoever you are.

While no-bake treats are a no-brainer when it's hot, don't let cooler temperatures stop you from enjoying delicious, easy-to-make, tempting goodies like my frozen fruit dessert (page 170), Blueberry Brownie Trifles (page 182), and Hot Fudge–Ice Cream Cone Pie (page 181).

I love adding whipped cream to a no-bake cheesecake batter until it's light and fluffy and ready to eat right out of the bowl. The Lime Cheesecake Mousse Cups (page 174), Chocolate Cheesecake Mousse Cups (page 169), and Berry-Swirled Cheesecake Mousse Bars (page 178) in this chapter are positively irresistible. You're also sure to be the most popular person in your home if you surprise your favorite cookie monster with Fully-Loaded Monster Cookie Dough Cups (page 173). And last but not least, the Peanut Butter–Banana Refrigerator Pie (page 165) has been called the greatest dessert of all time by more than one of the recipe testers who tried it. Yes, it really is that good.

PEANUT BUTTER–BANANA REFRIGERATOR PIE

Yield:
6–8 servings

Creamy peanut butter, hot fudge, whipped cream, and bananas combine with a chocolate cookie crust to make this positively amazing refrigerator pie. When I made this pie for the first time and took it to a potluck, people went absolutely crazy over it. This dessert has been overwhelmingly loved by everyone who tastes it.

FOR THE CRUST AND FIRST LAYER
12 chocolate sandwich cookies
3 tbsp (45 g) butter, melted
¾ cup (180 ml) Perfect-Every-Time Hot Fudge Sauce (page 156), room temperature, plus more for serving
2 bananas, sliced thin

FOR THE WHIPPED CREAM
1 cup (240 ml) heavy cream
1 tbsp (8 g) cornstarch
1 tbsp (7 g) powdered sugar

FOR THE FILLING
8 oz (230 g) cream cheese
1 cup (258 g) creamy peanut butter
1 tsp vanilla extract
1 cup (100 g) powdered sugar
¼ cup (60 ml) heavy cream

To make the crust and first layer, place the cookies in a large freezer-weight resealable bag. Use a rolling pin or mallet to crush them. Alternatively, you can quickly pulse them in a food processor. Combine the crumbs and the melted butter in a small bowl and stir to combine. Press the cookie mixture into the bottom of an 8 x 10–inch (20 x 25–cm) springform pan or a pie plate. Pour the fudge sauce over the crust. Place the bananas in a single layer over the fudge sauce.

To make the whipped cream, place the heavy cream in a medium bowl and beat with an electric mixer for 2 to 3 minutes, or until soft peaks form. Add the cornstarch and powdered sugar. Beat until firm peaks form. Transfer to a plate or small bowl and set aside.

To make the filling, combine the cream cheese, peanut butter, and vanilla in the same bowl used for the whipped cream. Beat for 2 minutes, or until smooth. Add the powdered sugar and beat for about 1 minute. Add the heavy cream and beat for 30 seconds, or until smooth and creamy. Use a spatula to gently stir in the whipped cream until combined.

Scoop the filling over the bananas. Spread with a spatula to form an even layer. Place the pie in the refrigerator and chill for at least 2 hours, or until firm. Slice and drizzle with hot fudge sauce before serving.

Baker's Note: This recipe can be made with homemade or store-bought hot fudge sauce. This can also be made in an 8-inch (20-cm) square pan and sliced into square bars.

COCONUT LOVERS' RICE-CRISPY BARS

Yield:
12–18
servings

Coconut lovers be warned, this bar is going to star in your food daydreams for years to come. I adore coconut and I also LOVE a great rice-crispy bar, so this combination is pretty much my idea of heaven.

While I'm admittedly a sucker for an amazing rice-crispy bar, not just any treat will do. If it's too hard and it scratches the roof of your mouth, that's just wrong. Falling apart in your hands? That is not cool. It needs to be just firm and sticky enough to hold together, yet soft and chewy and absolutely loaded with marshmallows.

6 tbsp (90 g) butter

10 cups (500 g) mini marshmallows (approximately 17 oz), divided

6 cups (168 g) crisp rice cereal

1½ cups (135 g) shredded sweetened coconut, plus extra for topping

Line a large baking sheet or a 9 x 13–inch (23 x 33–cm) pan with parchment paper. Feel free to use foil, if you'd prefer—just don't forget to grease the foil with butter to prevent sticking.

Melt the butter in a large pot, over medium heat. Add 8 cups (400 g) of the marshmallows and stir until they melt. Remove from the heat, add the cereal, and stir until combined. Stir in the remaining marshmallows and the coconut.

Scoop the sticky cereal mixture onto the lined pan. Use a lightly buttered spatula or spoon to gently press the mixture across the pan, being careful not to press too firmly. Sprinkle additional coconut over the top. Let it cool for a few minutes before slicing. Store in an airtight container for several days.

> *Baker's Note:* Don't press too hard when you are spreading this into the pan. Press as lightly as you can to spread them out. If you press them down too much, you'll wind up with a very firm rice-crispy treat, instead of perfectly stretchy, slightly sticky bars.

CHOCOLATE CHEESECAKE MOUSSE CUPS

Yield: 4–6 servings	Creamy chocolate cheesecake mousse is a perfect match for cherries and chocolate cookies. If these mousse cups are tucked into my refrigerator, the odds are good that you'll find my boys near them with spoons in hand.

½ cup (84 g) dark chocolate chips

¼ cup plus ⅔ cup (220 ml) heavy cream, divided

8 oz (230 g) cream cheese, room temperature

¼ cup (50 g) white sugar

½ tsp almond extract

½ tsp kosher salt

12 chocolate sandwich cookies, finely crushed

½ (15-oz [430-g]) can cherry pie filling

Combine the chocolate chips and ¼ cup (60 ml) of heavy cream in a glass bowl and microwave for 60 seconds, or until the chips are soft. Stir until smooth and glossy. Set aside.

In a medium bowl, place the cream cheese, sugar, almond extract, and salt and beat with an electric mixer for 2 minutes, or until smooth. Add the melted chocolate and beat until fully combined. Slowly add the ⅔ cup (160 ml) of heavy cream while beating constantly, for about 3 minutes. The mixture should be light and fluffy.

Divide half of the cookie crumbs between 4 to 6 small jars or bowls. Layer half of the cream-cheese mixture over the cookies and top with cherry pie filling. Repeat the layers until you are out of ingredients. Refrigerate for at least 1 hour, or until ready to serve.

Baker's Note: This recipe can also be assembled in one larger bowl and served family style.

FROZEN FRUIT DESSERT (AKA GRANDMA'S PINK STUFF)

Yield:
16–20
servings

When I was a child, we would often find a container of "pink stuff" waiting for us in Grandma McGinnis's freezer. She'd get it out after dinner, and we'd very happily dive in. Creamy, sweet, filled with bites of fruit, and absolutely irresistible, this is a frozen treat that we especially love on a warm summer night.

FOR THE STABILIZED WHIPPED CREAM
1 cup (240 ml) heavy cream
1 tbsp (8 g) cornstarch
2 tbsp (24 g) sugar

FOR THE FRUIT
8 oz (230 g) cream cheese, room temperature
¾ cup (150 g) white sugar
½ cup (120 ml) heavy cream
1 (20-oz [570-g]) can crushed pineapple, drained
12 oz (340 g) frozen sliced strawberries in juice, thawed
2 medium bananas, sliced thin

To make the whipped cream, place the heavy cream in a bowl and beat with an electric mixer for 3 to 4 minutes, or until soft peaks form. Add the cornstarch and sugar and beat for 2 minutes, or until firm peaks form. Scoop into a clean bowl, and set aside.

For the fruit, beat the cream cheese and sugar in the same bowl used for the whipped cream, until smooth. Slowly add the heavy cream while beating constantly. The mixture should be smooth and slightly fluffy. Add the pineapple. Beat to mix throughout. Add the strawberries along with all the juice and beat until well combined. Stir in the bananas. Fold in the whipped cream.

Pour into a 9 x 13–inch (23 x 33–cm) pan and freeze overnight. Once frozen, slice into bars. Serve immediately or store in an airtight container in the freezer for up to 3 months.

Baker's Notes: My grandma's original recipe included an 8-ounce (230-g) container of whipped topping. Feel free to swap that for the stabilized whipped cream listed in this recipe, if that's more your style.

Frozen sliced strawberries in juice are sometimes difficult to find at the store. To substitute fresh berries, combine 2 cups (332 g) of sliced strawberries with ½ cup (100 g) of white sugar. Stir to combine. Let the fruit rest on the counter while assembling the rest of this recipe. When the sugar has completely dissolved, add the fruit and all of the liquid to the recipe as directed above.

Variation: This dessert makes fantastic individual frozen treats. Freeze the mixture in fancy molds or in paper cups with a food-grade wooden stick or plastic spoon standing inside it.

FULLY-LOADED MONSTER COOKIE DOUGH CUPS

Yield:
8 servings

Everything you love about Monster Cookie Bars (page 93) is waiting for you in these completely snackable egg-free cookie dough cups. I've kicked this up a notch with some of our favorite add-ins, too. I'm willing to bet that you're going to love this cookie dough every bit as much as we do. I like to serve this cookie dough in small 4-ounce (115-g) jars. I've also been known to stash them in the back of the fridge for a sweet treat when the craving hits.

¼ cup (60 g) butter, softened

¾ cup (192 g) creamy peanut butter

¾ cup (150 g) light brown sugar

½ tsp baking soda

2 tbsp (30 ml) maple syrup

½ tsp vanilla extract

¾ cup (60 g) quick-cooking oatmeal

½ cup (84 g) chocolate chips

½ cup (84 g) M&M's candies

½ cup (84 g) mini peanut butter cups

½ cup (60 g) pretzel sticks, broken in thirds

In a large bowl, combine the butter, peanut butter, brown sugar, baking soda, syrup, and vanilla. Beat with an electric mixer or stir with a wooden spoon until creamy. Add the oatmeal and stir. Add the chocolate chips, M&M's candies, peanut butter cups, and pretzels and stir until combined. Scoop into airtight containers or jars.

Refrigerate until ready to eat. Bring to room temperature before serving, if desired. The cookie dough will keep well in the refrigerator for 1 week or in the freezer for 3 to 4 months.

Baker's Notes: The baking soda in this recipe is optional, but it adds a distinct "dough" flavor.

Old-fashioned rolled oats will work as well, if you do not have quick-cooking oats. The dough will have a more distinct texture, but I like both versions. If you are using rolled oats, increase the amount to about 1 cup (80 g). The dough should hold together, but should not be overly sticky. I prefer the rolled-oat version myself, but some of my family members prefer the slightly smoother smaller oats.

This recipe calls for the tiny peanut butter cups that are sold unwrapped in a bag, not the individually wrapped bite-size variety.

LIME CHEESECAKE MOUSSE CUPS

Yield:
6 servings

Light, refreshing, and sweetly tart, this is a dessert for the lime lover in your life. At first taste, the lime flavor won't be overly strong, but after a few hours in the refrigerator, the flavor will deepen and the lime taste will be perfection. Topped with fresh berries or Five-Minute Berry Sauce (page 160), the flavors are wonderful together.

FOR THE MOUSSE
8 oz (230 g) cream cheese, room temperature

½ cup (100 g) white sugar

1 cup (240 ml) heavy cream

½ tsp vanilla extract

¼ cup (60 ml) fresh lime juice

1½ tsp (2 g) finely minced lime zest

FOR THE CRUST
3 graham crackers, crushed into crumbs (approximately ½ cup [42 g]), divided

1½ tbsp (22 g) butter, melted

2 tbsp (25 g) light brown sugar

Fresh berries or Five-Minute Berry Sauce (page 160), for topping (optional)

Combine the cream cheese and sugar in a large bowl and beat until smooth. Slowly add the heavy cream while beating constantly with an electric mixer or the whisk attachment on a stand mixer. Beat until smooth and creamy and then continue beating for an additional 2 to 3 minutes, or until the mixture is fluffy. Add the vanilla, lime juice, and zest. Stir to mix well.

Combine the graham cracker crumbs, butter, and brown sugar in a medium bowl. Stir to mix until crumbs form. Divide half the graham cracker crumbs among the bottoms of 6 small ramekins or jars.

Divide the cream cheese mixture over the crumbs in the ramekins or jars, and then sprinkle with the remaining graham cracker crumbs. Top with berries or the berry sauce, if desired. Refrigerate for 2 to 3 hours before serving.

PRETZEL AVALANCHE FUDGE

Yield:
16–24 pieces

Rich chocolate, salty pretzels, and gooey marshmallows combine in this immensely snackable sweet-and-salty treat. Dark chocolate is my personal preference for these bars, as it makes the bars a little less sweet; however, my kids prefer the semi-sweet version. I've also made this recipe with white chocolate, and they're delicious that way too.

3 cups (504 g) semi-sweet or dark chocolate chips

1 (14-oz [420-ml]) can sweetened condensed milk

2 tbsp (28 g) butter

2 tsp (10 ml) vanilla extract

2 cups (240 g) mini pretzel twists

2 cups (100 g) mini marshmallows

Line a 6-cup (1.4-L) loaf pan with parchment paper.

Combine the chocolate chips, condensed milk, and butter in a medium glass bowl and heat in the microwave for 90 seconds. Stir to combine and heat another 15 seconds. Stir and heat an additional 15 seconds, only if needed. Stir until mostly smooth with just a few flecks of unmelted chocolate. Add the vanilla, pretzels, and marshmallows to the bowl. Stir to combine. Scoop the mixture into the prepared pan, and spread with a spatula.

Refrigerate for at least 4 hours before slicing into squares. Store in an airtight container in the refrigerator.

Baker's Note: This recipe calls for sweetened condensed milk, not evaporated milk, heavy cream, or half-and-half—nothing else will work. Trust me on this. Your fudge will not set if you use anything other than a can of sweetened condensed milk.

BERRY-SWIRLED CHEESECAKE MOUSSE BARS

<table>
<tr><td>Yield:
9–12 servings</td><td>Creamy, light cheesecake mousse swirled with berry sauce in a light graham cracker crust is worthy of any occasion. If you've never made a cheesecake, this is a fun one to begin with. Stir together the crust, mix the filling, and you're done. The hardest part is the waiting. In fact, even though the total hands-on time for this recipe is about 15 minutes, there is a bit of a wait for both baking the crust and chilling the filling. Yes, you can make a graham-cracker crust without baking it; however, a baked crust will have a sturdier texture and will be easier to cut and serve.</td></tr>
</table>

FOR THE CRUST
6 graham crackers, crushed
(approximately 1 cup [84 g])
2 tbsp (25 g) light brown sugar
¼ cup (60 g) butter, melted

FOR THE FILLING
12 oz (340 g) cream cheese, room
temperature
½ cup (100 g) white sugar
¾ cup (180 ml) heavy cream
2 tbsp (30 ml) fresh lemon juice
1 tsp vanilla extract
½ cup (120 ml) Five-Minute Berry
Sauce (page 160), room temperature
or cold

Preheat the oven to 350°F (177°C).

To make the crust, combine the graham crackers, brown sugar, and butter in a small bowl and stir to combine. Press the mixture into the bottom of an 8-inch (20-cm) pan. Bake for 10 minutes. Let it cool.

To make the filling, combine the cream cheese and sugar in a large bowl and beat until smooth. Slowly add the heavy cream while beating constantly with an electric mixer or the whisk attachment on a stand mixer. Beat until smooth and creamy and then continue beating for 2 to 3 minutes until the mixture is fluffy. Add the lemon juice and vanilla. Beat until smooth. Gently fold in the Five-Minute Berry Sauce, leaving plenty of swirls throughout. Pour into the cooled crust. Refrigerate for at least 8 hours, or overnight, before slicing and serving.

Baker's Note: Any berry sauce, chocolate, or caramel sauce may be used for the swirl in this recipe.

HOT FUDGE–ICE CREAM CONE PIE

Yield:
8 servings

My weakness for ice cream and ice cream cones is well-known. I love serving this pie to guests and then watching their faces as they try to figure out why it tastes exactly like an ice cream cone. Once you've made an ice cream cone crust, you're going to be hooked, and it just might change your ice cream game. You can make this pie with any ice cream you enjoy.

8 ice cream sugar cones or 6 waffle cones, broken into pieces

¼ cup (60 g) butter, melted

¼ cup (50 g) light brown sugar

1 cup (240 ml) Perfect-Every-Time Hot Fudge Sauce (page 156)

⅓ cup (80 ml) heavy cream

Vanilla or strawberry ice cream

Place the ice cream cone pieces in a food processor or blender. Pulse until the cones have broken down into fine crumbs. Combine the crumbs, butter, and sugar in a small bowl and stir to combine. Pour the crumb mixture into a pie plate or 8-inch (20-cm) pan and use your fingers to press it down to form the crust.

Place the hot fudge sauce and heavy cream in a small glass bowl. Microwave on high for 30 seconds. Stir until smooth and glossy. Drizzle half the warm hot fudge over the crust, covering as much of the crust as possible. Gently spread it across the crust with a spatula, as needed.

Carefully scoop freshly churned or slightly softened ice cream over the prepared crust. Smooth the top of the pie and drop spoonfuls of the remaining hot fudge over the top. Swirl lightly with a knife to mix throughout the ice cream. Place the pie in the freezer and chill for at least 2 hours before serving.

Baker's Note: Store-bought hot fudge sauce may be substituted for the homemade sauce listed in this recipe.

BLUEBERRY BROWNIE TRIFLES

Yield:
4 servings

Rich, fudgy brownie chunks are layered with juicy blueberries and fresh whipped cream to make these trifles. I highly recommend making a batch of the Blueberry–Chocolate Chunk Brownies (page 97) just for these trifles. Served in cute jars or glasses, this is a surprisingly easy dessert that is absolutely worthy of company.

FOR THE WHIPPED CREAM
1 cup (240 ml) heavy cream

2 tbsp (13 g) powdered sugar

½ tsp vanilla extract

FOR THE LAYERS
4 Blueberry Chocolate Chunk Brownies (page 97), chopped into bite-size pieces (approximately 3 cups [200 g])

1½ cups (222 g) fresh blueberries, divided

Shaved chocolate, for topping (optional)

To make the whipped cream, place the heavy cream in a bowl and beat with an electric mixer for 3 to 4 minutes, or until soft peaks form. Add the sugar and vanilla. Beat for 2 minutes, or until firm peaks form. Set aside.

To create the layers, place half of the brownie pieces in the bottom of 4 serving dishes. Divide ½ cup (74 g) of the berries over the brownies. Top with half of the whipped cream. Repeat the layers and top with the remaining berries. Garnish with shaved chocolate curls, if desired. Serve immediately.

Baker's Note: To shave the chocolate, run a vegetable peeler in short strokes along the edge of a bar of chocolate. The result will be lovely curls of chocolate. My preference for this recipe is a very dark chocolate, but any plain chocolate bar will work.

Acknowledgments

Sean: You are my rock, my heart, my other half. I wouldn't trade this life with you for anything.

Sam: This book wouldn't have happened without your willingness to work by my side in the kitchen. For all of the dishes you washed and the ingredients you prepped, thank you. You're going to get that queso cake one of these days. Just wait.

Ben: It's been a whole lot of fun watching you learn and grow this past year. I am immensely proud of you and the man you are becoming. You've made me a better parent, and I love you even more for that.

Nate: Your enthusiasm for tasting all the recipes in this book has brought so much joy to my heart. Thanks for reading to me, chatting with me, and never failing to provide your unique recipe insights as I tested these recipes.

To my family: Thanks for being my forever cheerleaders and supporting me endlessly. I love you all.

Rebecca: Thanks for the edits, the ideas, the endless parenting pep talks, the everything. I can hardly wait to live just 5 hours and 14 minutes from you.

To my girls: You are my people forever. There is no one else with whom I'd rather work, play, learn, and, most importantly, eat.

To my fellow bloggers: You inspire me every single day. This work that we are lucky enough to do, it's pretty amazing.

To the amazing group of home cooks who volunteered to test the recipes in this book: Thanks for sharing your feedback and helping make this cookbook all that it is. I can hardly wait for you to hold it.

To my local friends who were kind enough to taste test these desserts and take the abundance of desserts off my hands as I developed the recipes for this book: Thank you. Sharing food with friends is one of my favorite things, and your enthusiasm made writing this book so much more fun than I could've imagined.

To my readers: I am blessed every day to call you my friends. My life is a better place for having you in my corner of the internet.

Sarah, Will, and the whole team at Page Street: If you'd told me three years ago that we would work on three cookbooks together, I might not have believed it. I've enjoyed this work so very much. Thank you for everything.

"Taste and see that the Lord is good; blessed is the one who takes refuge in him." Psalm 34:8

About the Author

Mary Younkin is the creator, cook, and photographer for the recipe website Barefeet in the Kitchen. She is also the author of *The Weeknight Dinner Cookbook* and *The Weekday Lunches & Breakfasts Cookbook*. Millions of loyal readers have come to rely on Mary's recipes. Whether you're looking for breakfast, lunch, dinner, snacks, or dessert, the perfect recipe is waiting for you online or tucked into one of these cookbooks.

Nothing makes Mary happier than hearing that you've made her recipes and enjoyed them. She believes that recipes were meant to be shared, altered, passed around, and remade time and time again. Take these recipes and make them your own. Her hope is that you will love them as much as her family does. Mary lives in Granville, Ohio, with her husband, three boys, and an extensive collection of whisks and spatulas.

Index